FAITH MADE FLESH

A volume in the series

Publicly Engaged Scholars: Identities, Purposes, Practices

Edited by Anna Sims Bartel, Debra Ann Castillo, and Scott Peters

A list of titles in this series is available at cornellpress.cornell.edu.

FAITH MADE FLESH

The Black Child Legacy Campaign
for Transformative Justice
and Healthy Futures

**Edited by Lawrence "Torry" Winn,
Vajra M. Watson, Maisha T. Winn,
and Kindra F. Montgomery-Block**

CORNELL UNIVERSITY PRESS   ITHACA AND LONDON

Title Attribution: "Every Black child deserves to have a legacy" is from the poetic voice of Patrice Hill, a Sacramento artist, educator, and activist.

First published 2023 by Cornell University Press

Library of Congress Cataloging-in-Publication Data

Names: Winn, Lawrence T., editor. | Watson, Vajra, editor. |
    Winn, Maisha T., editor. | Montgomery-Block, Kindra F., editor.
Title: Faith made flesh : the Black Child Legacy Campaign for transformative
    justice and healthy futures / edited by Lawrence "Torry" Winn,
    Vajra M. Watson, Maisha T. Winn, and Kindra F. Montgomery-Block.
Description: Ithaca : Cornell University Press, 2023. | Series: Publicly engaged
    scholars: identities, purposes, practices | Includes bibliographical references
    and index.
Identifiers: LCCN 2023006801 (print) | LCCN 2023006802 (ebook) |
    ISBN 9781501772313 (hardcover) | ISBN 9781501772320 (paperback) |
    ISBN 9781501772337 (epub) | ISBN 9781501772344 (pdf)
Subjects: LCSH: Black Child Legacy Campaign (Sacramento, Calif.) |
    Racial justice—California—Sacramento. | Anti-racism—California—
    Sacramento. | Community activists—California—Sacramento. |
    African American children—Education—California—Sacramento.
Classification: LCC HT1561 .F358 2023 (print) | LCC HT1561 (ebook) |
    DDC 305.8009794/54—dc23/eng/20230426
LC record available at https://lccn.loc.gov/2023006801
LC ebook record available at https://lccn.loc.gov/2023006802

For our parents, our children, and our grandchildren who have yet to be born.
May the lineage of liberation guide your steps and carry you forward.
Always remember the land you walk upon
and honor those who, across time and space, nurture the pathway home.

The Word became flesh and dwelt among us.

—John 1:14

"Sethe," he says, "me and you, we got more yesterday than anybody.
We need some kind of tomorrow."

—Toni Morrison, *Beloved*

For the porch that Grandmama built.

—Kiese Laymon, *Heavy*

The Sacramento area was, and still is, the Tribal land of the Nisenan people. Sacramento is a gathering place for many local Indigenous Nations, including the Southern Maidu people to the north, the Valley and Plains Me-Wuk peoples to the south of the American River, and the Patwin Wintun peoples to the west of the Sacramento River.

> When we talk about land, land is part of who we are.
> It's a mixture of our blood, our past, our current, and our future.
> We carry our ancestors in us, and they're around us. As you all do.
> —Great-grandmother Mary Lyons, *Leech Lake Band of Ojibwe*

Contents

Acknowledgments

We would first like to acknowledge the parents and families of Black children living in the Sacramento region. Your efforts, dedication, and desires for promising futures for your children have not been lost during these uncertain times. We appreciate you! We also want to lift up all our essential workers: teachers and school leaders; community activists; city, county, and state employees; and everyone at nonprofit organizations advocating for better life chances and opportunities for children who are too often marginalized and silenced because of their race. Black children matter.

This book would not have been possible without the contributions of Damany Fisher, Ijeoma Ononuju, Patrice Hill, Quadir Chouteau, Kenneth Duncan, Heather Gonzalez, Amaya Noguera-Mujica, Adiyah Ma'at Obolu, David Gonzalez, and Vanessa Segundo. Fisher's expertise on the history of Black migration, residential redlining, and the disinvestments in Black neighborhoods provided the historical analysis needed to evaluate the effectiveness of the Black Child Legacy Campaign implementation strategy.

Adam D. Musser at *editing for change* was an invaluable partner who helped organize the book and prepare it for production. Vanessa Segundo, while a graduate student at the University of California, Davis, assisted with data collection and analysis, as well as drafting and designing key aspects of this book. We acknowledge technical assistance from the Transformative Justice in Education Center (UC Davis) and the College of Education at California State University, Sacramento. We also appreciate the support from the Sierra Health Foundation, namely Chet Hewitt, Leslie Cooksy, and Noemi Avalos who gave us access to data, people, and events.

We are grateful to Scott Peters, a professor in the Department of Global Development at Cornell University and faculty codirector emeritus of Imagining America: Artists and Scholars in Public Life. He was instrumental in helping shepherd this book from vision to reality. Likewise, Mahinder Kingra, the editorial director at Cornell University Press, was patient, gracious, and supportive every step of the way—thank you!

We would be remiss if we did not acknowledge that the Black Child Legacy Campaign itself was born out of struggle, preventable death, and pain. While writing this book, one of our coeditors experienced this grief when her nephew Santana Kane Harris (June 15–September 11, 2021) passed of SIDS in Sacramento.

While in mourning, the healers inside the Black Child Legacy Campaign—Heather Gonzalez, Brandi Missouri, and James Willock—grabbed hold and did not let go. Another BCLC partner, the Ramsey Wallace Funeral Home and Chapel, helped lay Santana to rest. This heartfelt network of compassion and care is firsthand testimony of our beloved community.

Finally, this book focuses on the work of the legacy builders and movement makers of Oak Park, Del Paso Heights-North Sacramento, Arden Arcade, North Highlands-Foothill Farms, Fruitridge Stockton Boulevard, Meadowview, and Valley Hi. To all the organizations and people representing these communities, thank you for the opportunity to observe, listen, learn from, and uplift your stories. We are forever grateful to you.

FAITH MADE FLESH

A CITYWIDE RECENTERING OF BLACK LIFE

Vajra M. Watson

The year is 2022. We are grateful to still be here. We remain inside multiple global pandemics and their physical, economic, environmental, educational, and social fallouts continue to amass. And yet, we realize that in times of collective sorrow *we find out who we are*. We find out what matters and what is trivial. We discover new points of connection and strength. We are able to look anew at our work and purpose.

As the editors and contributors of this book, we have been renewed and revivified by our study of a ten-year initiative in Sacramento, California, that centers Black families, Black leadership, and Black legacies. The foregrounding of racial justice has been a long time coming. We also know there is still a tremendous amount of work to be done.

To honor the journey thus far, we committed ourselves to sharing this invigorating story of Black Sacramento beyond our own city limits and the silos of the academy. In these pages, we invite you to listen and learn from scholar activists and movement leaders, youth practitioners and soul shakers, policy makers, and parents. Although distinct in perspective and positionality, this array of voices resounds in unison—like the future calling itself forward. The hymn is a remembering. A never forgetting. An envisioning. A call to action and a call to arms—arms that reach back, grab hold, and pull us together toward bolder possibilities. To a place where Black children survive and thrive. Have you been there, to the place that gloriously centers the Black race?

The Black Child Legacy Campaign (BCLC) offers a semblance of an answer. Its location offers its own lessons: we are offering a local case study with potentially

1

far-reaching implications about community–city–school partnerships. Guided by Black leaders, Sacramento became a hub of intersectional and intergenerational organizing within and across institutions. Centering Black life shaped all aspects of this work: from the formation of committees to funding streams, from selecting the seven neighborhoods to determining strategic priorities, goals, and outcomes. Intentionally selecting the word "legacy" connected the past to the future as the work took place in the present.

> They made us into a Race.
> We made ourselves into a People.
>
> —Ta-Nehisi Coates, *Between the World and Me*

The community-driven efforts and collective impact model of the BCLC are examples of what is possible for Black communities across the United States. But make no mistake: protecting and supporting the health and lifelong well-being of Black children is nothing new. Black people have been doing this work for centuries. We acknowledge these "solutionaries" who exist and resist in every city, on every farm, and in every neighborhood in this nation (Boggs 2013). These instrumental African American leaders are seeding, tilling, transforming, and growing new possibilities *right now*. We also know that many of those who are nourishing the soils of liberation go unnoticed, are undervalued, and are severely underpaid. For many, this work is not even their professional job. Rather, it is a duty, a calling, a way of being, and a way of life. It is in the rhythm of their justice walk, which attunes us to a hymn that reaches deep into the soul of this work. A connection that calls us home. These folks are everywhere, but their work is not always heard, respected, or connected.

> You never hear a tree grow.
> But you sure do see it blossom.
> Keep growing and lead by example.
> —Mistah F.A.B., "Keynote Address," May 19, 2017, UC Davis SAYS Summit

As in other communities across the country, in Sacramento, there were individuals doing "the work" long before the Black Child Legacy Campaign existed. Many folks tended to grind independently, some even antagonistically, with other organizations and institutions. There was a lot of divisiveness; people worked in "their area" with "their youth and families." A recipient of services shared, "It was all politics and poverty pimping." The environment in the 1990s and 2000s was bifurcated and siloed; everyone was clambering over the same dismal resources. Although there were genuine efforts and notable accomplishments during this time, they seemed piecemeal.

Based on an innovative strategy, the Black Child Legacy Campaign became a critical tool for alignment and a countywide beacon that would come to unify people intentionally, holistically, and powerfully. The collective actions of this innovative initiative are described in detail in the following chapters. But in this introduction, it is important to mention some essential seeds that made those achievements possible:

- The rigorous reallocation of resources totaling more than ten million dollars that were directed toward building the infrastructure of Black-led grassroots organizations.
- In each of the seven neighborhoods experiencing the greatest disparities in Black child deaths, the development of Community Incubator Lead organizations that became community resource hubs for supports and services to local residents.
- Cultural brokers who worked as a strategic bridge between families and multiple service agencies (like Child Protective Services and Probation).
- Crisis intervention response teams, which were often the first to arrive in an emergency, even before an ambulance or the police.
- The array of city and county departments that made the bold decision to place service providers directly inside community-based organizations, fortifying a wraparound model of commitment and care.

The groundswell of community support to do the work differently and disrupt traditional, inequitable, status-quo power dynamics ensured that Sacramento was fertile for innovation and growth.

Place Really Matters

Every city has a story, and every story can be told through race. What, then, is the history and present-day reality of white supremacy in a particular place? How do communities nourish racial justice? In Sacramento, Black leaders joined together as embodied in the BCLC to reimagine opportunities for their children in response to the visceral attacks on Black life.

Sacramento, the state capital of California, ranks high on several indices. It is heralded as one of the most multicultural places to live in the United States. In 2018, Sacramento was number six on the list of the most diverse large cities. In 2019, it ranked fourth for "ethnodiversity." Some may call Sacramento a true melting pot. Unfortunately, looks can be deceiving. We may witness the same sunset, but the horizons of opportunity are disproportionately different when measuring health, access, education, and equality.

Diversity does not mean equity. Here is the city that was forced to bury Stephon A. Clark (whose initials spell *SAC*).[1] Here is the city that continues to allow District Attorney Schubert and the police who fatally shot #StephonClark to continue their work. Here is the city where Black male students have the highest rate of suspensions in California. A comprehensive analysis of Sacramento reveals systemic underfunding and disinvestments in communities with predominantly Black families, which have led to dangerous racial disparities.

> If the youth are not initiated into the village,
> they will burn it down to feel its warmth.
>
> —African proverb

The divisive nature of racialized capitalism seeps through these streets; it is entrenched in the state capital. Disenfranchised and misguided African American youth did not wake up one day and start shooting at one another. Families do not intentionally put their babies to sleep in dangerous, life-threatening positions. Disproportionate data do not exist in a vacuum. As Chris Stewart makes plain in a July 20, 2020 article on Ed Post.com, "Just because you remove the leaves of racism, doesn't mean you've disturbed the root of it."[2] Building on this idea, in 2011, a wide range of stakeholders decided to hold the city accountable for equity outcomes.

In 2011, the Sacramento County Child Death Review Team revealed longitudinal data that shocked many but could not be denied: since 1990, Black children were dying at two to three times the rate of other children. The facts were enraging. Sacramento County Supervisor Phil Serna decided it was time to act aggressively to change this trajectory. He wrote to his fellow Board of Supervisors: "As a new county supervisor in 2011, I was alarmed to learn that in Sacramento County African American children die at very disproportional rates compared to other kids. I was even more distressed to know that little has been done to address this chronic problem despite the fact that it is something we've known about for decades."

Serna's advocacy led to the formation of the Sacramento Blue Ribbon Commission, which was to formulate recommendations for the Board of Supervisors to "address this chronic problem." The commission, comprising staff from First 5 Sacramento, the Sacramento County Department of Health and Human Services, and the Child Abuse Prevention Center, met for eighteen months. In 2013, it completed and disseminated a shocking public-facing report, *Disproportionate African American Child Deaths*.[3] It showed that it was not safe to be a Black infant or Black child in the capital of California. For many agencies—from the health system to child welfare—the inequalities it revealed were startling because the data were saturated with *preventive* factors. The four leading causes were identified as follows:

1. Infant sleep-related deaths
2. Perinatal conditions
3. Child abuse and neglect homicides
4. Third-party homicides

Even though the report and recommendations caused a countywide stir, systems are slow to change, and often the only action is to form another committee. Initially, this is exactly what happened in Sacramento: the County Board of Supervisors established the Steering Committee on Reduction of African American Child Deaths (SC-RAACD) to oversee the implementation of strategic interventions.

In theory, RAACD was to be a community-driven initiative with the aim of reducing deaths among African American children by 10 to 20 percent by 2020. The goal was ambitious, but African American children were in danger—literally. Even though the intention to achieve this reduction was real, policies and initiatives are only as strong as their people power and execution plan. Questions lingered about implementation. Who was going to *actually* make change happen? And how?

Our study offers answers through a layered analysis that carefully addresses the who and how of this work. Our multiyear examination is intentionally multifaceted, focusing on individual, interpersonal, and institutional inputs. The data demonstrate that the BCLC is nourishing neighborhoods with a community-based approach that is deeply rooted in a shared vision to improve the life expectancy of African American children and youth. Using this empowerment model, BCLC is providing a foundation that shows Black children how great they truly are and how mighty they can become.

> It's always at the top of my agenda to ensure Black children
> know their greatness through the past, but for others to know
> our greatness too. Because people can't see the greatness in you
> unless they know your history.
>
> —Community-based educator, Sacramento

Many powerful and positive changes have occurred throughout the region since the coalition with the deficit-based name, Reduction of African American Child Deaths, was re-envisioned as the Black Child Legacy Campaign. Between 2014 and 2017, the number of preventable Black childhood deaths dropped by 25 percent. Moreover, in 2018 and 2019, there were no third-party homicides in the county, which was unprecedented. "For twenty-eight months," recalls Chet Hewitt, president and CEO of the Sierra Health Foundation, "we went without a single homicide for anyone under the age of 18 within the city of Sacramento. That was the first time anyone's ever seen that happen." By 2020, Sacramento had far exceeded its original goal of reducing Black infant and child mortality.

The *Sacramento Observer*, in a 2021 profile of Hewitt, noted, "Today, in Sacramento, the Black Child Legacy Campaign (BCLC) is practically a household name, but sadly there was a time when the deaths of local Black children didn't get all that much attention."[4] Yet the success of the BCLC was largely informed by preexisting community-based solutions that heralded the fight for racial justice long before it was popular or there was funding for it.

Faith Made Flesh

Here is what I would like for you to know:
In America, it is traditional to destroy the black body—*it is heritage.*

—Ta-Nehisi Coates

Sacramento faces a typical American quandary: the realities of both white supremacy and Black power both run deep in the city. Yet, when we arrive at the corner where race meets place, a set of findings specific to Sacramento emerge. Throughout this book, we intentionally connect history to current-day possibilities and examine the ways this particular city reconciles with entrenched systems of institutionalized racism. Part of the work of this study is to unravel and deal with the historical, political, and racist nature of our city.

We intentionally oriented the focus of the study to move from this question— What are we fighting against?—to this one: *What are we fighting for?* To fully grasp this question in real time with real people, we connected Winn's transformative justice framework (2018) to the methodological use of portraiture (Lawrence-Lightfoot 1994; Lawrence-Lightfoot and Davis 1997; Watson 2012, 2014, 2018). Together, these tools sharpened the analysis and humanized the research journey. We offer language and leverage points to equip other scholars and organizers on this quest not only to study an issue but also to serve a community. We attempt to bring the work of the BCLC to life in this book by elevating community voices and complicated truths. We also aim to methodically provide wise witness to the impact and power of faith made flesh.

The old adage, "faith made flesh," was popularized on the 2020 HBO series, *Lovecraft Country.*[5] Sometimes art and popular culture intersect with academic research, and this historical horror-fantasy series (based on the novel by Matt

Ruff and developed by the Sacramento-born screenwriter and director Misha Green) carefully depicts both the living nightmare of the horrors of being Black in America and the power of intergenerational resistance.

Lovecraft Country is about persevering through the horrors of whiteness, white supremacy, and white vigilantism. It is about more than simply saving the series' protagonist, Atticus Freeman (played by Jonathan Majors); it is about remembering and futuring at the same time. It is a provocative, heart-wrenching telling of the power of community. The show demonstrates that our lives do not begin or end with us; they start long before we exist and end long after we transition—offering piercing, picturesque parallels to the Black Child Legacy Campaign.

One scene from Episode 9 ("Rewind 1921") is particularly significant for this book. To save her child, Atticus's Aunt Hippolyta (portrayed by Aunjanue Ellis) repairs a time machine and opens a portal to Tulsa, Oklahoma, in 1921, where Atticus and his companions witness the horrors of the Tulsa Race Massacre. There, they must retrieve *The Book of Names* before everything is consumed by the fire. This book, they believe, contains a cure that will awaken the child Diana from a curse; they are hopeful that it also contains a spell for protection from white folks and that the world will be set back right. When they find the book, the protagonist's grandmother hands it to Diana, saying, "When my great-great-grandson is born, he will be my faith turned to flesh."

"Faith made flesh" means turning a vision into reality, even if it takes generations. It may require a revolutionary fire that burns a path forward. How do we make a way when there is no way? We must catch the fire. And even if we cannot catch the fire for ourselves, may we at least ignite justice for our children and our children's children.

> Where is your fire? I say where is your fire?
> Can't you smell it coming out of our past?
> The fire of living . . . not dying
> The fire of loving . . . not killing
> The fire of Blackness . . .
> Where is our beautiful fire that gave light to the world?
> —Sonia Sanchez, "Catch the Fire"

The world is both sacred and scarred. The brutalities of inequity are looming and ever present. In July 2021, the Texas Senate passed legislation (S.B. 3) to end requirements to teach about women's suffrage and the civil rights movement: "Among the figures whose works would be dropped," Bloomberg News noted, are "Susan B. Anthony, Cesar Chavez, and Martin Luther King Jr., whose 'I Have a Dream' speech and 'Letter from a Birmingham Jail' will no longer make the curriculum cut."[6] On May 14, 2022, a white teenager goes on a livestreamed killing rampage of Black people at a grocery store in Buffalo, New York. In June 2022, Donald Trump hosts a "Save America" rally to celebrate recent Supreme Court rulings. At this gathering, Republican representative Mary Miller, of Illinois, hails the Supreme Court's decisions as a "historic victory for white life."[7] These acts of white supremacy do not exist in isolation: they are connected threads in a long line of patriots to the plantation.

Inside the United States, cities consistently perpetuate the status quo of racism. But there is another way. Poet Sonia Sanchez reminds us to hold light for ourselves and others. A decade ago, many leaders in Sacramento did not believe it was possible to stop or curtail the disproportionate preventable deaths of Black children and youth. The community saw it differently and committed to an ethic of consistent care and courageous cooperation that moved systems forward.

> In unity, a million threads can trap a lion.
>
> —Ethiopian proverb

The Black Child Legacy Campaign is more than a pocket of hope: it is a sustainable and replicable beacon of justice. To share this story effectively and holistically, my coeditors and I made the conscious decision to pivot and use our academic networks to develop a book that would elevate the insights of Black leaders, Black activists, and Black youth in Sacramento. Often missing from research are the direct accounts and analysis from the participants—those on-the-ground experts who share their truth in their own words. This does not mean that scientific inquiry does not have its place, but it is critical to understand the vitality and credibility of findings nurtured from the inside out.

We strategically center voice in this volume because people who embody the work of racial justice can be found everywhere. Our aim is that our singular and collective voices ignite a fire within you—*our reader*—and that the choir for change gets louder, uninhibited, and unapologetic in the quest for anticolonial realities. We imagine a policy maker in Seattle struggling to convince city officials to center the needs of Black families, or a group of youth activists in Mississippi building community gardens, or perhaps a schoolteacher in Toronto teaching about state-sanctioned police violence. We are calling you in—into this liberatory hymn.

Sacramento provides a kind of transformative torch, blowhorn, and blueprint through its bold citywide initiative, its policy shift, call to arms, funding streams, and comprehensive coalition of community well-being. It can be a catalyst for bolder horizons of radical possibilities. Horizons hold the rising and setting of the sun. Horizons hold time, symbolizing intersections between imagination and reality. The horizon is also a meeting place between sky and earth, between past ancestry and future humanity. We argue that it is imperative to engage in the beautiful struggle while also working to liberate the public from fatalistic renderings of Black life. Liberatory futures center Black legacies, transforming theory to practice and our faith into flesh. We each have a calling, a fire that paves the way. We want you to know that you matter because we matter, and the work of a new world implicates all of us.

> If you have come here to help me,
>
> you are wasting your time.
>
> But if you have come
>
> because your liberation is bound up with mine,
>
> then let us work together.
>
> —Dr. Lilla Watson, Murri (Aboriginal Australian) activist

NOTES

1. Local students created a spoken word piece to educate the world about Stephon A. Clark. Watch it here: https://www.youtube.com/watch?v=I5LocKrncM4.

2. Chris Stewart, "What if Your Entire School System Was the Racist Monument that Should Come Down?" Ed Post.com, July 20, 2020. https://educationpost.org/what-if-your-entire-school-system-was-the-racist-monument-that-should-come-down/.

3. Blue Ribbon Committee, *Disproportionate African American Child Deaths*, May 7, 2013. https://www.thecapcenter.org/admin/upload/BOS%20Blue%20Ribbon%20Presentation.pdf.

4. Genoa Barrow, "Chet Hewitt: Q&A," October 27, 2021. https://sacobserver.com/2021/10/chet-hewitt-qa.

5. I want to thank Marvin Reed, a doctoral student at Sacramento State, for being a thought partner and having lively, insightful discussions about *Lovecraft Country* with me.

6. Paul Stinson, "Texas Senate Votes to Remove Required Lessons on Civil Rights," July 26, 2021. https://news.bloomberglaw.com/social-justice/texas-senate-votes-to-remove-required-lessons-on-civil-rights.

7. Becky Sullivan, "A GOP Congresswoman Said the End of Roe Is a 'Historic Victory for White Life,'" June 26, 2022. https://www.npr.org/2022/06/26/1107710215/roe-overturned-mary-miller-historic-victory-for-white-life.

REFERENCES

Boggs, Grace Lee. 2013. "Solutionaries Are Today's Revolutionaries." *Boggs Blog*. October 27, 2013. https://conversationsthatyouwillneverfinish.wordpress.com/2013/10/27/solutionaries-are-todays-revolutionaries-by-grace-lee-boggs/.

Coates, Ta-Nehisi. 2015. *Between the World and Me*. New York: Spiegel & Grau.

De Ley, Gerd. 2019. *The Book of African Proverbs: A Collection of Timeless Wisdom, Wit, Sayings & Advice*. New York: Penguin Random House.

Lawrence-Lightfoot, Sara. 1994. *I've Known Rivers: Lives of Loss and Liberation*. Reading, MA: Addison-Wesley.

Lawrence-Lightfoot, Sara, and Jessica Hoffmann Davis. 1997. *The Art and Science of Portraiture*. San Francisco: Jossey-Bass.

Mistah F.A.B. 2017. "Keynote Address." May 19, 2017. UC Davis SAYS Summit.

Sanchez, Sonia. 1995. *Wounded in the House of a Friend*. New York: Penguin Random House.

Watson, Lilla. 1985. Speech given at the United Nations Decades for Women Conference. Nairobi, Kenya.

Watson, Vajra M. 2012. *Learning to Liberate: Community-Based Solutions to the Crisis in Urban Education*. New York: Routledge.

Watson, Vajra. 2014. *The Black Sonrise: Oakland Unified School District's Commitment to Address and Eliminate Institutionalized Racism*. Final evaluation report submitted to Oakland Unified School District's Office of African American Male Achievement. http://www.ousd.org/Page/12267.

Watson, Vajra. 2018. *Transformative Schooling: Towards Racial Equity in Education*. New York: Routledge.

Winn, Maisha T. 2018. *Justice on Both Sides: Transforming Education through Restorative Justice*. Cambridge, MA: Harvard Education Press.

THE ROADMAP
We Make the Path by Walking

Lawrence "Torry" Winn

Between 2017 and 2020, Vajra Watson, Maisha Winn, and I collaborated on an evaluation for the Sierra Health Foundation and its Black Child Legacy Campaign (BCLC). Initially, we were hesitant to take on this study because we each were in the middle of several ongoing educational research projects and had timelines to meet. However, there was something special about BCLC that we could not deny: its name "Black Child Legacy." We were attracted to the words "Black," "child," and "legacy." As educational researchers, we were all too familiar with titles and names of projects, organizations, and programs that were deficit oriented. But the name "Black Child Legacy" was brilliant. We were also drawn to BCLC because it was community driven and connected seven Black neighborhoods. Although BCLC was the hub, its spokes reached all parts of the community: nonprofits, government entities, law enforcement, families, and schools. Vajra, Maisha, and I all agreed that we needed to use our academic training and university resources to assist with telling the story of the BCLC and its desire to build bright futures for Black children. We decided to use a humanizing (respecting the community and individuals) and transformative (getting to the root problem of a cause to bring about sustainable change) framework that highlighted BCLS's successful practices and programs and analyzed its efforts that were not working.

During the three-year evaluation process, our research team (including our graduate research student Vanessa Segundo) met bimonthly with the Sierra Health Foundation and its leadership team: Chet Hewitt, CEO; Leslie Cooksy, evaluation director; and Noemi Avalos, evaluation associate. Kindra

Montgomery-Block, the fourth editor of this book, was employed by the Sierra Health Foundation and oversaw the BCLC initiative. Her leadership was critical to its sustainability. As we heard stories from participants, learned about the inner workings of the neighborhoods, and observed community leaders, we decided to provide an opportunity for the community leaders, youth, and participants to share their experiences with the BCLC in a book.

In fall 2021, we sent out a call for proposals to community members to write either a research-theory based chapter or a reflection essay about their experiences. We emailed, posted, and shared the call for proposals with community organizations to recruit contributors. Those who answered the call and whose work is included in this volume are as follows:

- *The historian*: Damany Fisher, a Sacramento native and the son of the founders of Shule Jumamose (an independent Black institution established for the educational futures of Black children), is a University of California, Berkeley–trained historian and an expert on redlining and housing discrimination in Sacramento.
- *The spoken word artist/educator*: Patrice Hill is a poet, public speaker, youth advocate, host, curator, community-based educator, and the current director of Sacramento Area Youth Speaks. Patrice has more than two decades of experience teaching in urban, suburban, and exurban communities. She is the featured artist in BCLC's poetic service announcement: "Every Black Child Deserves to Have a Legacy."
- *The youths*: Adiyah Ma'at Obolu and Quadir Chouteau are both high school student poets and activists. Adiyah states, "I create my own poetry as a way to honor my story and the future I want to create for the world." Their high schools and communities have been and continue to be affected by gun violence.
- *The BCLC community leaders*: Ijeoma Ononuju, a PhD graduate of the School of Education of the University of California, Davis; Kenneth Duncan, a social justice advocate and founder of Ball Out Academy; and Heather Gonzalez, director of the Mutual Assistance Network write about their on-the-ground experience of community leadership.
- *The community artist*: David Blanco Gonzalez grew up in the Oak Park neighborhood of Sacramento. He began drawing as a young child and as a teenager was influenced by hip-hop and graffiti art. He was commissioned by the Black Child Legacy Campaign to create his first collection called "Legacy" to pay respect to the victims of third-party homicide in Sacramento and talk about the process of using art as a tool for healing.

- *The health and wellness advocate*: Amaya Noguera-Mujica, an employee of the Sierra Health Foundation, passionately highlights the need to acknowledge racism and oppression and their impact on health and wellness.

The Path Forward

"Part I. Legacy" in chapter 2, provides a summary of the social, historical, and political contexts of the Black Child Legacy Campaign and the events that led to the launch of this citywide effort. It also describes the framework of five pedagogical stances—history matters, race matters, justice matters, language matters, and futures matter—and the research methods used to evaluate BCLC. Chapter 3 shows how *history matters* by tracing the history of racist policies in real estate and housing that contributed to the current problems in the Black community in Sacramento, which was once referred as a utopia for Black people. It concludes with portraits of seven Sacramento Black communities.

"Part 2. Learning" demonstrates the ways in which *race matters* in Black education. Chapter 4 highlights the Black educational initiatives and schools aimed at creating pride and instilling Black values in Black children. In chapter 5, the educator and poet Patrice Hill reflects on her time in the classroom as a teacher. A youth poet, Quadir Chouteau, shares his experience of being Black in high school and the impact that gun violence has on learning in chapter 6, and chapter 7 speaks to the significance of being a Black community educator outside the walls of the school. Offering principles for leaders involved in community building, chapter 8 describes how community leaders applied these lessons after a local youth was murdered.

"Part 3. Leadership" provides examples of lessons learned by BCLC leaders doing *justice matters* work. Chapter 9 grapples with the question of how an outsider comes into a community and builds capital to effectively serve as a BCLC Community Incubator Lead. Chapter 10 establishes the founding of Build. Black., Sacramento's foremost inclusive community economic development collaboration, which was created after the death of Stephon Clark and subsequent community meetings with the Sacramento government and the Sacramento Kings, the NBA team.

"Part 4. Life" emancipates and unfolds the fullness of the humanity of the individuals involved in the BCLC. Through the portraits of Phil, Chet, Kindra, Crystal, and Jackie, we can show, not just tell, the intimate and intricate nature of movement building. In this section, the author's pay close attention to the words and stories shared highlighting language matters and is important to cultivating life.

"Part 5. Lessons" provides the opportunity for three community leaders to share their personal experiences with BCLC and the editors to outline the lessons and findings from its evaluation, which can provide best practices for other municipalities considering collective impact and using a community-driven model. It concludes with the coeditors' focus on *futures matter.*

Part 1
LEGACY

"Part 1. Legacy" provides the social-historical-political context of the Black Child Legacy Campaign and the events that led to the launch of a citywide effort. Torry Winn, Maisha Winn, and Damany Fisher illustrate why *history matters* to understanding the current conditions and state of Black communities and how history can be used as a tool to transform the future for Black children. In chapter 2, Maisha and Torry Winn present their framework of "5 Pedagogical Stances"—*history matters, race matters, justice matters, language matters,* and *futures matter*—and the methods used for the evaluation. Damany then outlines the history of racist policies in real estate and housing that contributed to current problems in the Black community.

TRANSFORMATIVE JUSTICE FRAMEWORK

Building Black Legacies

Maisha T. Winn and Lawrence "Torry" Winn

During the spring and summer of 2020, millions of individuals across the world stood in solidarity to protest oppressive, dehumanizing policies and practices that harm Black lives. A movement sparked by the deaths of George Floyd, Breonna Taylor, and Ahmaud Arbery—on top of so many other Black deaths in recent years—highlighted pervasive racial inequities that affect the life chances and opportunities of African Americans, as well as Indigenous, Latinx, and other historically marginalized communities. In a matter of months—though these overdue changes were decades in the making—states and cities removed Confederate flags, monuments, and statues; universities and museums renamed buildings previously honoring white supremacists; food companies discontinued the use of racist images and stereotypes; hundreds of private business and philanthropic foundations agreed to invest billions of dollars into organizations focused on anti-Blackness and improving the quality of life for Black families; and cities such as Asheville, North Carolina, began providing reparations for African Americans in under-resourced communities.

The pursuit of racial justice spread to every corner of the world: from Minneapolis to London, from Tokyo to New York, from Portland to Washington, DC. In Sacramento, thousands joined weekly protests led by local activists, leaders, youth, and organizations to oppose unfair justice systems and racial policies in the region. Established and emerging leaders held bullhorns and led chants of "Black Lives Matter" and "No Justice, No Peace." Protests moved from Oak Park to Greenhaven to Natomas. Rallies led by Black youth and leaders included individuals and groups representing diverse industries, ages, demographics, and ethnicities. Sacramento City Unified School District's Board voted to end its contract with school resource officers, and Sutter Medical Center removed a statue of colonizer John Sutter.

The deaths of George Floyd, Breonna Taylor, and Ahmaud Aubery were not the only catalysts for action against anti-Blackness and police brutality. The devasting impacts of COVID-19 had already shed light on the racial disparities of historically marginalized communities and particularly for those who are Black, Indigenous, and People of Color. In places like New York City, Chicago, New Orleans, and Atlanta, African Americans were infected and died at a disproportionately higher rate than their white counterparts (Grace, Johnson, and Reid 2020). Similar data emerged in Arizona and New Mexico for the Navajo Nation and in cities such as Los Angeles and San Jose for the Latinx community. In Sacramento, communities such as Oak Park, South Sacramento, and Del Paso Heights, where large numbers of African Americans reside, experienced high infection rates.

Yet, the fight against injustices that harm Black children and their families and communities, with a core focus on addressing the causes and impacts of racial health disparities, did not begin in 2020. The Sacramento region has experienced and pushed back against decades of state-sanctioned violence toward Black adults and youth. In the spring of 2018, Sacramento communities, leaders, and activists marched for justice after a police officer fatally shot Stephon Clark in his grandmother's backyard. Sacramento has lost hundreds of Black lives to gun violence, inadequate access to health care, and other avoidable causes. Local organizations have advocated for years to address these injustices.

The Black Child Legacy Campaign (BCLC) was a bridge connecting pre- and post-COVID-19 and pre- and post-Black Lives Matter protests. Its work with community organizations, leaders, residents, and families before COVID helped pave the foundation for a strong community response. BCLC's efficient and expansive network was years in the making (see figure 2.1).

Background

In April 2013, the Sacramento Blue Ribbon Commission *Report on Disproportionate African American Child Deaths* presented data documenting twenty years of disproportionate African American child mortality in Sacramento County, recommended the adoption of the goal of reducing African American child deaths by at least 10–20 percent by 2020, outlined potential approaches to achieving the goal, and established the Steering Committee on the Reduction of African American Child Deaths (SC-RAACD). The report identified the four causes

FIGURE 2.1. 2020 Steering Committee on Reduction of African American Child Deaths (Sierra Health Foundation).

Credit: Terence Duffy.

of death most disproportionately affecting African American children in Sacramento County: infant sleep-related deaths, perinatal conditions, child abuse and neglect homicides, and third-party homicides.

The report also highlighted neighborhoods with the most disproportionate rates of African American child death in the county. Seven neighborhoods became the focus of the efforts of the SC-RAACD: Arden-Arcade, Del Paso Heights/North Sacramento, Fruitridge/Stockton Boulevard, Meadowview, North Highlands/Foothill Farms, Oak Park, and Valley Hi. Within these communities, the aim was the strategic provision of targeted resources to bring about urgently needed systemic changes and improve the health and well-being of the most vulnerable children.

After an intensive community process driven by core values of collaboration, community engagement, commitment, accountability, innovation, sustainability, and service, the Steering Committee created a strategic plan in March 2015, "African American Children Matter: What We Must Do Now," outlining five priority strategies to transform public systems and foster meaningful community engagement:

1. advocacy and policy transformation
2. equitable investment and systematic impact
3. coordinated systems of support

4. data-driven accountability and collective impact

5. communications and information systems

In June 2015, the Sacramento County Board of Supervisors voted to approve $1.5 million annually for five years to support implementation of the strategic plan. This funding commitment supplemented investments by the county's First 5 Sacramento Commission and its public health, human services, child welfare, and probation departments. The funding from the Board of Supervisors was structured to focus on engaging community and both building and strengthening community infrastructure to quickly mobilize to reduce the specific causes of death cited in the Blue Ribbon Commission's 2013 report. In 2016, the City of Sacramento joined the initiative, committing $750,000 in the first year. Additional funding was since obtained from other sources, including the Obama Foundation, First 5 Sacramento, and the Board of State & Community Corrections for a total of $10.9 million (2014–2020).

Shortly after receiving funding from the Board of Supervisors, the Steering Committee issued an implementation plan that described how the five interdependent strategies would be put into operation. Seven community organizations were selected as Community Incubator Leads (CILs) to coordinate and implement services and communications at the neighborhood level. Respected within their communities, the CILs are responsible for strengthening community infrastructure to ensure that the changes created by the initiative are sustainable. The CIL's were assisted by the Community Leadership Roundtable, which comprised of residents who volunteer in the seven neighborhoods.

Evaluating the BCLC Strategies Using a Transformative Justice Framework

In July 2018, together with Vajra Watson, we began a two-year evaluation of BCLC. The members of our research team were selected for their academic prowess and long-standing ties to Sacramento. The purpose of the evaluation was threefold. It examined how the SC-RAACD implemented the five strategies in seven designated neighborhoods to reduce African American child deaths, identified the challenges and promising practices highlighted during implementation, and determined how best to scale up this work in other jurisdictions and communities experiencing similar issues throughout the United States.

From July 2018 through July 2020, the evaluation team examined multiple sources of data, including stakeholder interviews, participant-observation of the

Steering Committee's Evaluation Workgroup meetings, observations of several other Steering Committee meetings, and review of archival documents. The analysis of BCLC's implementation of the five strategies was guided by these four research questions:

1. In what ways and to what extent has each strategy been implemented?
2. What are the challenges to and facilitators of implementation success?
3. How, if at all, are Steering Committee strategies influencing public systems and their relationships with community organizations?
4. How, if at all, are Steering Committee strategies strengthening communities in ways that are likely to reduce African American child death and sustain low rates of African American child deaths into the future; for example, through increased CIL capacity, reduction of risk factors for the four causes of death, or improved utilization of services?

Design, Data, and Positionality

The design of the evaluation was transformative, participatory, and ethnographic, linking qualitative data to the quantitative data on changes in the rates and disproportionality of African American child death. Ethnographic research appropriately maintains a "focus on the lived experiences, activities, and social context of everyday life from the perspectives of the participants" (Mertens and Wilson 2018). The research team used several data collection methods that are culturally responsive and not "damaged centered" (Tuck 2009). The evaluation approach was multidimensional and considered microlevel individual impact points in relation to macrostructural system shifts. Thus, examining data points at the personal, interpersonal, and institutional level informed the findings.

Methodology

The evaluation used the following methods:

Participant observation: Participant observations were conducted to fully participate and learn about the implementation of the five strategies, thereby providing a deeper understanding of the implementation process. The researchers immersed themselves in the culture and social functions being evaluated through daily routines, practices, and meetings.

Qualitative interviews: Qualitative interviews were conducted with selected participants and stakeholders. They were semi-structured, using an open-ended protocol that invited narrative responses and encouraged participants to speak openly about their personal experiences with the challenges, successes, and promises of strategy implementation.

Data analysis: Field notes were analyzed by first writing conceptual memos, which helped organize the findings and bring in theoretical insights that emerged during engagement in the field. Patterns and themes emerged from the field notes and observations and provided the words and phrases used subsequently for coding categories (Bogdan and Biklen 1997). Interviews were transcribed and analyzed for "significant statements," which were organized into themes (Creswell and Poth 2016).

Historical analysis: The disproportionality of African American childhood deaths in Sacramento did not develop randomly, recently, or in isolation. To study this crisis without an accurate understanding of its relevant historical context would be intellectually inappropriate. Thus, the research team conducted a historical analysis using archival data of the communities participating in BCLC; it also did a public policy review to shed light on histories of homeownership, community investment, social services, and education, unemployment, and poverty rates. This information allowed us to look at how history matters to patterns of child death.

Positionality

> A transformative approach to justice . . . addresses the harms and obligations inherent in social, economic, and political systems.
>
> —Howard Zehr

The evaluation focused on cultural competency, a commitment to community-driven solutions, and an emphasis on structural and historic barriers. The evaluator's research was grounded in transformative justice beliefs:

- We believe evaluators/researchers must resist conducting "damage-centered" evaluations/research in Indigenous and marginalized communities (Tuck 2009). The seven neighborhoods have been historically marginalized, racially segregated, and economically oppressed. As researchers who come from similar communities, we know firsthand the damage of deficit-based interventions.
- We believe in "humanizing research" in which scholars become "worthy witnesses" in their sites by earning the respect and trust of participants (Paris and Winn 2013). We have collectively written more than one hundred articles, books, chapters, and reports that discuss participants as experts rather than objects/subjects.

- We believe *history matters*, *race matters*, *justice matters*, *language matters*, and *futures matter*—and must be examined and explicitly addressed to get to the root of inequities (Winn 2018).
- We believe that the aim and approach of the Black Child Legacy Campaign align seamlessly with our own work and goals to ensure that every child, especially those from marginalized communities, enjoys the access, support, and opportunity to live healthy and prosperous lives.

Transformative Justice Framework: Five Pedagogical Stances

The researchers use a transformative justice framework, adopted from Maisha T. Winn's (2018) "5 Pedagogical Stances" (5PS), to evaluate the Black Child Legacy Campaign:

History matters is a pedagogical stance that draws attention to local, national, and global histories. It calls on communities to find ways to engage the histories and lived experiences of those who comprise the BCLC community. The next chapter presents a history of race and real estate in Sacramento that provides context for the various neighborhoods and shows how systemic racism through redlining and zoning can affect generations. *History matters* is also a call for people to historicize their own lives while connecting to the histories of others, so that there can be a collective understanding of how our lives intersect, as well as the lives of our families and communities.

Race matters is a pedagogical stance inviting stakeholders in a community to see the full humanity and potential in people while actively resisting racist ideas that impede one's ability to cultivate a connection or relationship. *Race matters* is also affirming. In the BCLC's work, race/ethnic identity and pride serve as guides through transformative conversations about how race, racism, and racist ideas show up in services the community needed.

Justice matters is a pedagogical stance that encourages stakeholders in a community to consider how social movements seeking equity across domains such as education, the workforce, health care, and ownership map on to their communities. In the BCLC, the distributed leadership seen in Community Incubator Leads (CILs) is an example of how justice projects are often launched by everyday people who identify an issue and take action. The BCLC story offers examples of how people with different areas of expertise and lived experience come together on behalf of Black children, Black families, and Black life.

Language matters is an invitation for communities to consider the role of language in defining/redefining and illuminating the assets people bring to the community, rather than situating people and their experiences as burdens or deficits. For example, the use of "legacy" rather than "infant mortality" is at the heart of this story. When the BCLC team came together to imagine how it would look and sound different than similar efforts throughout the country, the deliberate use of the word "legacy" provided a map and a compass for the work. This pedagogical stance is a commitment to the importance of interrogating language and ensuring it does not hold anyone hostage by its limitations.

Futures matter is a pedagogical stance that is deeply committed to ensuring that there are determined and desirable futures for children and their families. In many ways, *language matters* and *futures matter* work side by side in the BCLC story: a clear focus on legacy is a commitment to Black futures. How do we provide Black children and their families with tools to imagine their lives ten years from now? What legacy/legacies can Black children and their families imagine when they are confident in their futures and in their ability to plan for and execute futures they desire?

A Transformative Evaluation Process

As transformative evaluators, we expect their social justice values to influence the process and outcomes of their evaluation work (Mertens and Wilson 2018). While conducting the evaluation, it soon became apparent that the stories, experiences, and contributions of the participants needed to be explored in greater detail. Even though the research design, data collection, findings, and future implications are the backbone of this book, its soul is grounded in community contributions and celebrations. We researchers listened, observed, and studied the actions of the BCLC participants. The story of the BCLC would not be complete without reflections written by members from the community, portraits of several leaders, and chapters authored by African American residents of Sacramento County. It is through their lived experiences, stories, and faith in a better future that the data become flesh.

REFERENCES

Bogdan, Robert, and Sari Knopp Biklen. 1997. *Qualitative Research for Education.* Boston: Allyn & Bacon.

Creswell, John W., and Cheryl N. Poth. 2016. *Qualitative Inquiry and Research Design: Choosing among Five Approaches.* 4th ed. Thousand Oaks, CA: SAGE.

Grace, De'zhon, Carolyn Johnson, and Treva Reid. 2020. "Racial Inequality and COVID-19." *Capitol Weekly,* May 4, 2020. https://capitolweekly.net/racial-inequality-and-covid-19/.

Mertens, Donna, and Amy T. Wilson. 2018. *Program Evaluation Theory and Practice: A Comprehensive Guide.* 2nd ed. New York: Guilford.

Paris, Django, and Maisha T. Winn, eds. 2013. *Humanizing Research: Decolonizing Qualitative Inquiry with Youth and Communities.* Thousand Oaks, CA: SAGE.

Tuck, Eve. 2009. "Suspending Damage: A Letter to Communities." *Harvard Educational Review* 79, no. 3, 409–428.

Winn, Maisha T. 2018. *Justice on Both Sides: Transforming Education through Restorative Justice.* Cambridge, MA: Harvard Education Press.

Zehr, Howard. 2015. *The Little Book of Restorative Justice.* Rev. ed. New York: Simon & Schuster.

HISTORY MATTERS

Realities of Redlining in Sacramento

Damany Morris Fisher

Sacramento County's disproportionately high rate of Black child deaths can be traced to the city's historic practice of residential segregation and redlining, which is the refusal by lenders to give mortgage or home improvement loans to qualified borrowers in high-risk, typically declining neighborhoods. However, it is also important to recognize that African Americans in Sacramento and their allies have a long history of civil rights activism and community mobilization to fight back against these practices. Just as they mobilized in response to Stephon Clark's killing at the hands of Sacramento police in 2018, Black Sacramentans waged a vigorous, decades-long campaign against residential segregation. Just as the NAACP argued its case against racial segregation in public schools in the landmark case of *Brown v. Board of Education* in 1954, the Sacramento branch of the NAACP targeted federally insured housing that excluded African Americans from new suburban neighborhoods. Just as the lunch counter sit-ins, Freedom Rides, the Birmingham campaign, and the March on Washington captured national attention in the early 1960s, civil rights activists in Sacramento picketed in front of the offices of real estate developers and engaged in civil disobedience to force California lawmakers to pass fair housing legislation. The Black Child Legacy Campaign (BCLC) is heir to this legacy of resistance and struggle.

Despite the gains made from this campaign for fair housing, institutionalized racism in Sacramento's housing market made it difficult for many Black families to accumulate generational wealth. At the same time, neighborhoods like Del Paso Heights, Oak Park, and Meadowview, which collectively housed most of the city's African American population, suffered from disinvestment and neglect caused by years of redlining. Not coincidentally, the *Report on Disproportionate African American Child Deaths* identified these communities as among those with the highest African American child mortality rates in Sacramento County.

The Origins of Residential Segregation in Sacramento

Despite its allure and reputation as a land of boundless opportunity for African Americans, Sacramento, much like the rest of California, did not always live up to its billing. The vast majority of African Americans remained trapped in the service sector, working in restaurants, hotels, hospitals, and train stations. Black carpenters and other skilled tradesmen were denied membership to local unions or guilds, making it difficult for them to practice their trade. Black women, meanwhile, found few prospects outside domestic work. Housing proved no less of a challenge for Black Sacramentans. Restrictive covenants and other measures methodically kept Blacks out of most Sacramento neighborhoods while confining them to older, deteriorating areas like downtown Sacramento's West End (De Graaf, Mulroy, and Taylor 2001; Somerville 1949).

Blacks first settled in the West End in the 1850s and remained concentrated there well into the twentieth century. This pattern did not result accidentally but rather through coercion. Convinced that African Americans and non-whites threatened property values and the quality of life, white real estate agents and property owners used whatever means available to restrict Black mobility. The most often used and effective means were informal agreements between real estate agents and property owners not to rent or sell houses to Blacks; Sacramento real estate agents continued to steer African Americans into areas that already had a Black population.

Another practice of homeowners and realtors, which became particularly widespread in the 1920s, was the use of racially restrictive covenants: these barred homeowners from selling or leasing their property to African Americans and other non-whites, usually for a period ranging from twenty to thirty years (Hirsch 1992; Massey and Denton 1993). As in other cities, this combination of informal agreements and racially restrictive covenants in Sacramento locked African Americans out of many neighborhoods.

Postwar Migration and the Beginning of the Fair Housing Movement in Sacramento

During the 1940s and 1950s California became one of the main arenas for organizing around fair housing and equal employment. The "Double V" campaign—victory over fascism abroad and racism at home—spearheaded by the *Pittsburgh Courier* during World War II inspired African Americans and their allies to redouble their efforts to end Jim Crow in the United States and force the nation to live up to its creed of equality. This spirit fueled a surge in membership in the Sacramento NAACP, which, by the late 1940s, possessed the energy, capacity, and resources to demand better housing and jobs in the city. Reflecting the diverse range of Sacramento's expanding Black population, its campaign included everyone from university-trained professionals to city sanitation employees. It also involved a growing number of Black military personnel stationed at McClellan and Mather Fields. Some had come from communities with a strong tradition of civic engagement, political organizing, and self-advocacy. As in other cities, many brought these traditions with them to communities like Sacramento during the Second Great Migration (see table 3.1).

Still, the absence of Black attorneys who could take up civil rights cases continued to be a frustrating reality. That changed in 1948 with the arrival of Nathaniel Sextus Colley. Born and raised in Snow Hill, Alabama, Nathaniel Colley graduated with honors from Tuskegee University in 1941. Despite being turned away from the University of Alabama law school after serving in World War II, Colley was admitted to Yale University. Graduating near the top of his class in 1948, several universities offered him teaching posts. Colley, however, decided to relocate to Sacramento, his wife's hometown. This marked an impor-

TABLE 3.1   African American population and percentage of overall population in select California cities, 1940 to 1970

CITY	1940	%	1950	%	1960	%	1970	%
Los Angeles	63,774	4.2	171,209	8.7	334,916	13.5	503,606	17.9
Oakland	8,462	2.8	47,562	12.4	83,618	22.8	124,710	34.5
Sacramento	1,468	1.4	4,538	3.3	12,103	6.3	27,244	10.7
San Diego	4,143	2.0	14,904	4.5	34,435	6.0	52,961	7.6
San Francisco	4,846	0.8	43,502	5.6	74,383	10	96,078	13.4

Note: The total Black population for Sacramento's Standard Metropolitan Statistical Area (SMA) in 1950 stood at 7,499; in 1960: 19,805; in 1970: 37,911.

Source: Steven Ruggles, Katie Genadek, Ronald Goeken, Josiah Grover, and Matthew Sobek, *Integrated Public Use Microdata Series: Version 6.0* [Machine-readable database] (Minneapolis: University of Minnesota, 2015).

tant turning point in the civil rights struggle in Sacramento, which at the time had no practicing Black attorneys. Colley helped transform the Sacramento NAACP into a more effective organization, winning several suits on behalf of Black victims of police brutality and various forms of racial discrimination (Nathaniel Sextus Colley, interview). In 1951, the West Coast Regional Office of the NAACP (NAACP-WC) designated Colley as the legislative representative of the NAACP for the state of California. The following year he helped form the NAACP-WC Regional Legal Redress Committee, along with attorneys Loren B. Miller and Terry Francois. ("N.A.A.C.P. West Coast Regional Reorganization Conference" 1951, National Association for the Advancement of Colored People, Region I, Records, BANC MSS 78/180 c, Bancroft Library, University of California, Berkeley). By the early 1950s Colley had distinguished himself as a brilliant lawyer and champion of civil rights not only in Sacramento but also throughout the region.

River Oaks Campaign, 1951–1952

"As California's civil rights struggles moved beyond legalized segregation," according to the historian, Mark Brilliant, "the state was at the forefront of fair housing litigation and legislation" (Brilliant 2010, 5). The NAACP West Coast Region, based in San Francisco, was often at the center of this fight, litigating several cases in the 1940s and 1950s that yielded important victories against segregation in both public and private housing. Loren Miller, based in Los Angeles, served as the NAACP's expert on housing cases; he collaborated with Thurgood Marshall to prepare briefs and oral arguments for the Supreme Court's 1948 ruling in *Shelley v. Kraemer*, which held that restrictive covenants that prohibited the sale of property to non-whites violates the equal protection clause of the Fourteenth Amendment. Under Miller's leadership, the NAACP and other civil rights organizations "brought an avalanche of complaints about housing restrictions to the courts" (Hudson 2020, 200–201). At the grassroots level, many NAACP chapters organized campaigns pressuring city authorities and real estate boards to adopt nondiscrimination policies.

To provide relief to struggling families and to address the city's acute housing needs, Sacramento city officials, with assistance from the Public Works Administration (PWA) and the United States Housing Authority (USHA), constructed four public housing projects by 1944: New Helvetia, Dos Rios, Parker Homes, and Defense Dormitories at Grant Union High School. The PWA and the USHA issued directives that guaranteed African Americans a certain number of public housing units and construction jobs. Both required local municipalities to follow a "neighborhood composition guideline," which guaranteed that the process of tenant selection in the earliest projects did not depart from local residential patterns. As a result, local housing authorities often limited access to units for non-whites and insisted on strict segregation within each project (Hirsch 2000, 161). Sacramento City Housing Authority officials did not deviate from this pattern. It not only denied Black families their fair share of housing units but also confined them to all-Black areas in developments like New Helvetia; even so, only 16 or 310 units there had Black occupants, and Dos Rios had no Black residents. The proportion of units allocated to African Americans did not reflect their housing needs. (Sacramento City Council Minutes, January 3, 1952; "City Will Probe" 1952). Given this context, civil rights organizations believed that targeting discrimination in public housing first made the most practical sense.

The construction of the River Oaks housing project created an opportunity for civil rights organizations to confront the Sacramento City and County Housing Authority, which had jurisdiction over the city's public housing. In December 1951, the Sacramento Chapter of Democratic Action and the Sacramento NAACP met with commissioners from the Housing Authority and implored them to change their segregation policy. In response, Albert H. Becker, executive director of the Sacramento City and County Housing Authority, announced that housing units in Dos Rios "will be made available to minority race families" for the first time. Becker also pledged to increase the "quota" of units designated for minority groups at New Helvetia and River Oaks. He revealed that it was "true" that the housing authority enforced a policy of racial segregation, but he contended that "there has been no discrimination against making housing available to these groups" ("Dos Rios Homes" 1951). When pressed by civil rights groups to put these new policies in writing, Becker refused to do so. Despite being threatened with legal action, he remained defiant: "There isn't anything you can do in court . . . Legally you people haven't a leg to stand on" (Mayer 1953).

Becker's refusal to guarantee changes to existing policies convinced civil rights activists to step up their pressure campaign. On December 29, 1951, a multiracial coalition of civic and religious organizations met and formed the Committee against Segregation in Public Housing. Committee members explored various strategies, including litigation. Nathaniel Colley, head of the committee's legal counsel, believed that litigation could be an effective tool but "costly" if the case went to trial with one or more appeals to higher courts. Therefore, Colley recommended legal action only as a "last resort" (Mayer 1953, 30) Ultimately, the committee focused its efforts on the new River Oaks project, hoping to block any attempt from the housing authority to impose the same racial segregation policy there that already existed in New Helvetia. "We have got to start [such action] somewhere," said Colley, "It is obvious that once Negroes are moved into lily-white areas in one housing project, the whole policy of racial segregation has been broken down" ("Housing Heads Surrender" 1952).

Overturning that policy, however, would prove difficult. When the committee presented a resolution opposing segregation to the City Council, it refused to vote on it and instead forwarded it to the city manager, Bartley Cavanaugh. Cavanaugh told the committee that while he favored integration, he exercised little influence over the Housing Authority. it did something "absolutely illegal," said Cavanaugh, the City Council "stayed out of the housing business." (Mayer 1953, 28) As the Committee against Segregation in Public Housing quickly surmised, the city council and housing authority had a vested interest in maintaining the status quo. Both bodies remained beholden to the local real estate establishment. Where the City Council was concerned, the adoption of a resolution opposing segregation in public housing had broader implications. If it opposed segregation in public housing, how could it then condone segregation in private housing?

Once it became clear to the Committee against Segregation in Public Housing that the Housing Authority remained committed to maintaining separate Black and White units at River Oaks, it decided to pursue legal action against city officials. Wary of bad publicity, the Housing Authority chose to reevaluate its segregation policy (Mayer 1953). On January 31, 1951, it changed course, declaring that henceforth "Negro families will be assigned, as accommodations become available, to units in any part of the project regardless of the race of families occupying adjoining or nearby apartments." It further declared that thirty-two of the sixty-four Black families scheduled to move into River Oaks would be asked to "defer occupancy until a later date" to ensure that "strict integration" could take place ("Integration Policy" 1952). The Committee against Segregation, however, rejected the commissioners' plan and accused them of trying to buy more time while they continued to segregate current and new Black residents, creating what it described as a "Black Belt" within the project. Colley explained to committee members that if occupation was to be deferred, it would become nearly impossible to present a case to a judge that on its surface appeared to be a "satisfactory arrangement."

On February 1, 1952, Colley filed suit in the Sacramento County Superior Court on behalf of three Black River Oaks tenants: Willie Franklin, Marion Reynolds, and Norma Johnson. According to the suit, they had been assigned to special buildings in the one area restricted to Black occupants. The suit also alleged that "defendants [city officials] threaten to deny Plaintiffs admission to said project unless Plaintiffs consent to be segregated therein solely because of their race or color." This would violate the "Charter of the United Nations, the

Constitution of the United States, Section 1978 of the United States Code, the Constitution and public policy of the State of California and the National Housing Act of 1937 and 1949." That same day, the Superior Court judge signed an order preventing the Sacramento Housing Authority from moving any Black families into segregated units until the case for integration could be presented ("Groups Sue to Prevent" 1952).

In the following month, the Housing Authority, under continued pressure from activists and the courts, again announced plans to "make a good faith effort to carry out a policy of racial integration." It agreed to give the sixteen Black families the option of moving from segregated units to ninety units still under construction that would include White families. Although some committee members praised the plan, others raised questions, particularly with respect to the provision that gave the Housing Authority discretion over the "administrative details" of the transfer. The agency's history of reneging on previous agreements inspired little confidence among many committee members (Mayer 1953, 33). As it turned out, the Housing Authority did everything possible to discourage Black families from moving, such as requiring them to pay all moving-related expenses, denying them access to moving trucks, and, in some instances, refusing to issue them keys to new units. Even though all the families were relocated by late April, they were still relegated to "segregated knots." Instead of moving Black families next to whites, the Housing Authority arranged for them to be placed in units next to Mexican Americans, Chinese Americans, and Japanese Americans. When Canson and West accused Becker of chicanery, he told them that "Mexicans" were, in fact, "Caucasians." One frustrated tenant, Elmo Williams, summed up the collective feeling of the committee when he said, "This isn't what I thought of as integration" (Mayer 1953, 40). By April, the Committee against Segregation in Public Housing disbanded, with many of its constituents uncertain about whether it had been successful. Even though the Housing Authority publicly proclaimed its commitment to integration, its efforts to enforce this policy can be described as token at best.

Despite the Housing Authority's intransigence, the committee's goal of dismantling segregation in public housing was ultimately achieved. In the case of *Banks v. Housing Authority of the City and County of San Francisco*, the Regional Legal Redress Committee represented Mattie Banks, a single Black mother, who was denied a unit in an all-white housing development. NAACP attorneys accused the city of maintaining a racial quota system in violation of the Fourteenth Amendment. On September 1, 1952, San Francisco Superior Court Judge Melvyn I. Cronin declared the neighborhood guideline policy "illegal and void" and an "unlawful violation of the Fourteenth Amendment and the laws and general public policy of the State of California and the City and County of San

Francisco" (Broussard 1993, 224). He argued that, in light of the 1948 *Shelley* decision, the Housing Authority's policy of excluding Black tenants from certain housing units "should not apply to a public housing project, financed by public funds and supervised by a public agency." The Constitution, Cronin stated, applied to the individual, not to a specific race or group; therefore, the "neighborhood pattern" policy of selecting tenants was unconstitutional. The District Court of Appeals upheld the Superior Court's ruling in 1953, and the U.S. Supreme Court declined to hear the case. This decision gave the Regional Legal Redress Committee its first major victory and the "first victory on the appellate level in the United States on the question of public housing" (Brilliant 2010, 143). As Miller later wrote, the decision "was taken to mean that the separate-but-equal rule had no application to public housing" (Broussard 1993, 225). This victory helped establish the reputation of the NAACP West Coast Region as the leading civil rights organization in the state.

The River Oaks campaign underscored the determination of local government—via the Sacramento City and County Housing Authority—to maintain the city's color line in public housing, and, by extension, all housing. Yet the River Oaks, *Banks*, and other housing cases provided momentum to the fair housing movement in Sacramento and gave the NAACP the opportunity to hone its legal strategy for the next phase in the struggle for fair housing: eliminating racial discrimination in federally assisted *private* housing.

The Fair Housing Ordinance, 1954

After the *Banks* decision, the Sacramento NAACP turned its full attention to fighting discrimination in private housing. One of its strategies used the controversial issue of redevelopment to pressure the Sacramento City Council to adopt a citywide fair housing ordinance. Since the early 1900s, Sacramento downtown business elites had complained of deteriorating conditions in the West End and urged that the area's aesthetics be improved and its economic vitality restored. In 1954, the Sacramento Redevelopment Agency introduced its redevelopment plan—the Capitol Mall Project—to the public. Many West End residents and community groups opposed the project because it called for the demolition of their homes and businesses. For these people, the West End was not the slum that it was being portrayed as by government officials and the press. It was home to a thriving Japanese American community still reeling from the impact of wartime incarceration. It was also home to many working-class African American families who—confronted by the reality of racial discrimination in housing—had few options available to them. If the West End was demolished, where else in the city could they live?

Representatives from the African American, Asian American, and Latino American communities urged the City Council to adopt measures that dealt fairly with West End residents. Sensing an opportunity, the NAACP decided to pressure the city to adopt a citywide ordinance banning discrimination in private housing. On September 16, 1954, attorney Douglas R. Greer, chair of the Special Committee on Urban Redevelopment for the Sacramento NAACP, presented the City Council with a proposed ordinance calling for "the prevention of discrimination in ownership, use and occupancy of real estate in the City of Sacramento" ("Law Banning Realty Racial Laws" 1954). It guaranteed all people living in the city of Sacramento "equal opportunity to purchase, own, occupy, lease and sub-lease real property . . . without discrimination or segregation on account of race, color, creed, or national origin" (NAACP, Proposed City, 1954). City Manager Cavanaugh told the Council he saw nothing "objectionable" in the proposal and seemed to offer support for its adoption. The City Council, however, quickly moved to postpone any consideration of the ordinance until October 7, 1954.

Ultimately, the City Council refused to implement a citywide fair housing ordinance. Instead, it passed a nonbinding resolution that only *recommended* that every redevelopment plan forwarded to it for approval contain "adequate provisions precluding direct or indirect discrimination . . . or segregation" in deeds, leases, and contracts ("N.A.A.C.P. Endorses Redevelopment" 1954). Despite being disappointed by the council's decision, the NAACP pledged its support for the Capitol Mall Project. "We've been for redevelopment as a principle all along," Colley told the *Bee*, "and have held back endorsement of this particular program because we wanted to see [if] certain safeguards were provided. The resolution adopted last night provides those safeguards." Still, Colley made it clear to the City Council that the NAACP's citywide ordinance proposal was "still on the memorandum list" and was "much more desirable" ("City Bans Discrimination" 1954; "N.A.A.C.P. Endorses Redevelopment" 1954).

Ming v. Horgan, 1954–1958

Although the City Council did not pass a fair housing ordinance, the NAACP continued its campaign against racial discrimination in federally assisted private housing. As early as 1952, the Regional Legal Redress Committee made its services available to any NAACP branch that targeted racial segregation in private housing with FHA/VA commitments (NAACP, Minutes of Meeting, 1952). The committee initially looked toward the San Francisco Bay area and Los Angeles for its test cases before settling on one in Sacramento County in which African Americans had been routinely turned away from new housing

FIGURE 3.1. Front page of the *Sacramento Outlook* on May 21, 1954. The NAACP filed its suit against a group of Sacramento area developers the same week that the U.S. Supreme Court issued its ruling in the landmark *Brown v. Board of Education*.

Source: Nathaniel S. and Jerlean J. Colley Papers, Center for Sacramento History.

developments. On May 10, 1954, the legal committee of Colley, Miller, and Williams filed suit on behalf of Oliver A. Ming, a Black World War II veteran and McClellan Field employee, and nine other African Americans against several of the largest real estate and construction firms operating in the county (see figure 3.1).

According to the suit, on January 15, 1954, Ming had attempted to purchase a home in McClellan Meadows, a subdivision located in the North Highlands neighborhood. Even though Ming met all qualifications, the NAACP charged that the real estate broker, Milton G. Horgan, refused his application solely on account of his race. Other defendants named in the suit included the Sacramento Real Estate Board (SREB), McBride Realty Company, Hackes & Hurst Real Estate, and more than a dozen individuals. Collectively, they had built or sold virtually all the units in Sacramento County since 1944. The suit accused the defendants of having conspired to refuse to sell homes to African Americans. It claimed that the National Housing Act of 1934, which created the FHA, was passed by Congress for the purpose of providing affordable housing to citizens of the United States "without distinction as to race, color or creed." The suit charged defendants of ignoring new FHA guidelines that had gone into effect on February 15, 1950, which denied mortgage insurance to builders who failed to pledge not to apply race-restrictive covenants to their developments. Such actions, according to the plaintiff, violated both the National Housing Act of 1934 and California state law. The plaintiff asked the court to nullify the so-called oral agreement among the defendants and prohibit them from refusing to sell homes to Blacks "except upon terms and conditions applicable alike to all citizens, regardless of race, creed, or color" ("Suit Charges Race Bias in Area Housing" 1954).

Coming in the wake of the 1954 *Brown v. Board of Education* decision, many felt that the *Ming* case marked the next logical step forward for the civil rights movement. Speaking at a press conference, Franklin Williams announced that "the two greatest discriminatory practices remaining" in California were "housing and employment bias" ("NAACP Head Hits Housing, Hiring 'Evil'" 1955).

On June 23, 1958, Judge Oakley handed down a decision in favor of Oliver Ming. He concurred with the plaintiff's argument that the National Housing Act of 1934 sought to provide adequate housing for all Americans who met certain financial requirements, regardless of race. Because every law passed by Congress contained an inherent antidiscrimination clause, Oakley declared, the FHA could not "play favorites as to race, color, or creed" and had an obligation to extend the benefits of such legislation to all qualified citizens. Although developers and real estate agencies reserved the right to discriminate on the basis of race when carrying out exclusively private business, the fact that they operated under the auspices of the federal government when receiving mortgage loan guarantees obligated them to accord *all* applicants the same rights.

Judge Oakley's 1958 ruling in the *Ming* case had far-reaching implications not only in the state of California but also throughout the nation. It marked the first successful legal challenge to racial discrimination in private housing built with FHA/VA commitments and the first court-ordered injunction requiring builders and developers to cease their practice of not selling homes to African Americans ("Negroes on Coast Win Housing Case" 1958; "Rules out Biased Home Deals" 1958). Most importantly, *Ming* opened the door to legislation in California prohibiting racial discrimination in all publicly assisted housing. The 1958 election of Democrat Pat Brown to the governorship and the corresponding ascendance of liberal politics in the state during the late 1950s and early 1960s led to a legislature that was more receptive to civil rights (Flamming 2000).

After more than a decade of legislative battles and pressure from civil rights organizations, Governor Brown finally signed the long sought-after California Fair Employment Practice Act on April 16, 1959, which banned "discrimination or abridgement on account of race, religious creed, color, national origin, or ancestry" in employment. The law would be enforced by the newly created Fair Employment Practice Commission (FEPC). That same year, Governor Brown also signed into law A.B. 890, known as the Hawkins Act, which forbade racial discrimination in "publicly assisted" housing in California. This legislation, however, had severe limitations: it only applied to builders who used federal or state mortgage insurance and not to homeowners, who could still refuse to sell or lease their property to anyone based on race (Brilliant 2010).

Fair Housing in the 1960s

Unfortunately, the *Ming* decision came too late to reverse decades of residential segregation in Sacramento. By 1960, restrictive covenants, redevelopment, and adverse government policies created a landscape in which the vast majority of Blacks remained clustered in Oak Park and Del Paso Heights. This residential segregation did not go unnoticed. In December 1960, the Sacramento Council of Churches organized a symposium on "minority housing conditions" in the Sacramento area for clergy, realtors, academics, and civic leaders. After touring several neighborhoods and interviewing residents, participants concluded that "redevelopment of the west end has led to a concentration of Negro families in Oak Park." Reverend W. Morgan Edwards, pastor of the First English Lutheran Church in Oak Park, observed that the Black student population at American Legion School Park had climbed from 12 percent in 1952 to 50 percent in 1960. "When redevelopment first started," Edwards said, "one redevelopment representative said, 'If any large portion of this population in the west end concentrates in another area, we will have failed.' Well, I can assure them they have failed." The symposium also found that African Americans who purchased homes in Sacramento suburbs were typically required to make a down payment up to three times higher than that paid by whites. The only plausible explanation for such disparities in Sacramento's housing market, the symposium concluded, was race (Littlewood 1960).

These revelations inspired some symposium participants to take action. Included among this group was Leonard Cain, professor of sociology at Sacramento State College, who cofounded the Sacramento Committee for Fair Housing (SCFH) in 1961. One of its first actions was to publish a report titled *Housing Discrimination in Metropolitan Sacramento*; this was the first detailed analysis of residential segregation in Sacramento to draw from census data. It noted that real estate firms, lending agencies, and home sellers were primarily responsible for contributing to patterns of segregation, which constitute "a major barrier to the utilization of opportunities available to most citizens." The Oak Park, Del

Paso Heights, and Glen Elder neighborhoods accounted for approximately half of African Americans living in the Sacramento metropolitan area. By contrast, northeast Sacramento County, which included the districts of Arden-Arcade, Carmichael, Fair Oaks, Citrus Heights, and Orangevale—not coincidentally, areas where the vast majority of FHA-insured housing was built—had only 42 Blacks of a population of 71,356, or less than 0.06 percent. "It is abundantly clear," the report concluded, "that Oak Park has replaced the redeveloped West End as Sacramento's new downtown Negro community, with a concentration of Negroes not previously experienced in the West End" (Cain 1961, 1–3). African Americans in Sacramento had charged local realtors of "racial steering" for decades; the report's analysis provided irrefutable support for their claims.

Fair housing advocates in Sacramento saw their movement as one more battlefront in the national struggle for racial equality and one that was no less important than the protests then taking place in the South. "The prospect that the battle for desegregation will be won in the South at the very time it is being lost in other parts of the nation, primarily through discriminatory housing practices, is a sobering prospect indeed," Cain wrote. "It can happen; it is happening in Sacramento" ("S.S.C. Prof Says Segregation in City Increases" 1961). The realization that housing discrimination flourished in Sacramento and the dramatic example of nonviolent protests sweeping across the South inspired Sacramentans to get involved in the Black freedom movement (see figure 3.2). New organizations like the SCFH joined existing organizations such as CORE in drawing attention to challenges Blacks faced in securing decent housing. The multiracial SCFH drew from a cross section of academics, civic, and religious leaders "to help insure equality of opportunity for housing for all persons of metropolitan Sacramento without regard to race, religion or national origin" ("Fair Housing Committee Plans to Elect Officers" 1961).

Federal intervention notwithstanding, more far-reaching legislative reform took place at the state level. On February 14, 1963, California assemblyman W. Byron Rumford introduced A.B. 1240, which extended prohibitions against racial discrimination in publicly assisted housing to all private housing. The bill designated the Fair Employment Practice Commission as the administrative body to enforce the law. Violators faced misdemeanor charges, resulting in imprisonment for six months, a $500 fine, or both. From the moment it was introduced during the legislative session, the so-called Rumford Act touched off intense debate.

Fair housing activists championed the measure and mobilized to pressure the legislature to pass it. On March 27, more than 400 people from Sacramento and across the state packed the hearing rooms of the State Capitol where the Committee on Governmental Efficiency and Economy was seeking public comment

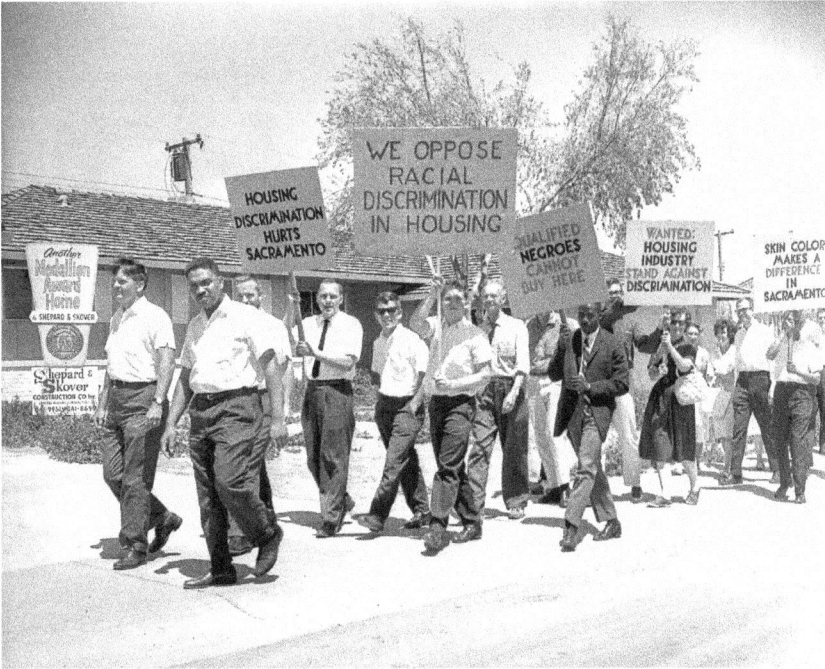

FIGURE 3.2. Members of the SCFH protesting housing discrimination in South Land Park Hills on June 9, 1962.

Source: Sacramento Bee Collection, Center for Sacramento History.

about the proposed legislation. Several witnesses testified in favor of the law, warning that housing discrimination in California contributed to urban decay and social disorder. Opponents of the measure insisted that A.B. 1240 violated individual property rights and that it would do little to advance civil rights ("Fair Housing Bill Following Argument" 1963; "Housing Bill Clears Committee" 1963; "Housing Bill Goes to the Assembly Floor" 1963). The next day, a dozen Black and white CORE members from across the state staged a sit-in at the capitol, promising to remain until the legislature passed the Rumford Act; this demonstration lasted twenty-four days (see figure 3.3; "Race Equality Body Stages Capitol Sit-In" 1963). Rumford and several of his supporters, including the NAACP, expressed concern about CORE's action, fearing that such a move would alienate state legislators and therefore reduce support for the Rumford Act. The NAACP preferred to work within the system and negotiate with state legislators, and many of its older members regarded the actions of CORE and other civil rights organizations as potentially harmful to the civil rights cause. CORE, meanwhile, grew increasingly impatient with the impasse over the Rumford Act (Casstevens 1967).

FIGURE 3.3. CORE members occupying the rotunda of the California State Capitol in Sacramento on May 28, 1963.

Source: Sacramento Ethnic Communities Survey, Center for Sacramento History.

Despite strong opposition from the real estate industry and many Republican legislators, the California state legislature passed the Rumford Act on June 21, 1963. The final version prohibited racial discrimination in all publicly assisted single-family homes and apartments of five or more units; that is, those receiving VA, FHA, or Cal-Vet financing or located within a public housing or redevelopment project ("Rumford Act's Aim Is Clear: To Block Discrimination" 1963; "State Fair Housing Bill Is Passed" 1963).

The law authorized the FEPC to investigate and resolve complaints of alleged racial discrimination. If that failed, FEPC commissioners could hold a public hearing and award up to $500 to victims of housing discrimination. Even though the legislation only applied to one-third of the state's housing, the Rumford Act was one of the most comprehensive fair housing laws passed in the postwar era (Brilliant 2010, 192). It was not to remain in effect for long, however.

Many African Americans in California viewed the battle over Proposition 14—a ballot measure that amended the California state constitution to nullify the 1963 Rumford Fair Housing Act—as a litmus test of the state's attitude toward civil rights. Therefore, when California voters overwhelmingly passed the proposition on November 3, 1964, by a two-to-one margin, many African Americans expressed shock and disillusionment. "California today has no fair housing law. It has in reality legalized second-class citizenship," wrote the *Sacramento*

Observer. "It is truly a sad day in California's history" ("Salvaging the Good" 1964). Blacks who had migrated from other states felt particularly dejected because they had been led to believe that conditions in the state would allow them to lead fulfilling lives unencumbered by the blatant racism in the South and other parts of the nation. One such individual who moved from Ohio to Sacramento a decade earlier wrote a letter to the *Observer* claiming that he felt "psychic trauma" on receiving news that Californians decided to "constitutionalize" housing discrimination ("California Secedes from the Union" 1964).

It was no coincidence that, after the California electorate overturned the Rumford Act, the Black community in Watts exploded during the summer of 1965. Although it became known as the "Watts Riot," to many observers it resembled more of an "uprising"—a reaction to decades of intense residential segregation and police brutality. The NAACP attributed it to "continued practices of racial discrimination and segregation in housing, employment, education and in every other phase of American life" (NAACP West Coast Region 1965). The clashes in Watts underscored the failure of the civil rights movement to eliminate structural inequality in housing and employment (Horne 1997). Preventing "another Watts" became a rallying cry for fair housing and antipoverty organizations.

On May 10, 1966, the California State Supreme Court declared Proposition 14 unconstitutional because it violated the Fourteenth Amendment. The court maintained that the Fourteenth Amendment, through the equal protection clause, provided every individual the right to acquire and possess property "of every kind without discrimination because of color, race or religion." Individuals, therefore, could not discriminate for "personal economic or social considerations." The Supreme Court agreed. On May 29, 1967, the Supreme Court, in a 5–4 decision, upheld the California Supreme Court's decision in *Reitman v. Mulkey* that Proposition 14 was unconstitutional (Casstevens 1967, 82–84). The Supreme Court's ruling marked an important victory for the fair housing movement in California, secured after decades of local organizing and mobilization in communities across the state. In pursuing "distinctly local agendas," fair housing activists in Sacramento became catalysts for changes at the state and federal levels to outlaw racial discrimination in public and private housing.

Urban Crisis

"All manner of evils trail in the wake of residential segregation," stated the NAACP West Coast Region in 1954. "High incidence of crime, juvenile delinquency and disease can be correlated with overcrowding and bad living conditions that are inevitable results of the exclusion of Negroes, and other so-called non-Caucasians, from all but limited sections of our towns and cities." For the NAACP and many civil rights organizations in the urban North and West, racial discrimination in housing represented the greatest challenge to social and economic justice for African Americans (NAACP, Region I, Records, Freedom's Frontier 1954). When introducing the NAACP's fair housing ordinance in 1954 to the Sacramento City Council, attorney Douglas Greer had argued that unless the city guaranteed equal access to housing to all its residents, new slums would simply replace those located downtown. His prophecy was fulfilled.

By the late 1960s and early 1970s, Oak Park and Del Paso Heights were symbols of urban crisis. The flight of middle-class Whites and businesses from Oak Park, for example, left those communities in economic ruin. In 1973, the *Sacramento Union* described Del Paso Heights a "city apart," replete with substandard housing, inadequate services, and despair (Lee and Lee 1973). Bank redlining left Oak Park and Del Paso Heights mortgage deficient and starved of needed capital and resources (Department of Savings and Loan 1979; Dingemans 1979). Indeed, the infrastructure of both districts had deteriorated to the point where each became the target of belated redevelopment efforts by the city in the 1970s; they proved, ultimately, unable to reverse decades of neglect and decline.

A Deeper Look: Portraits of Each BCLC Neighborhood

Although the neighborhoods that are the focus of the BCLC's efforts each have a unique history, they share threads of divestment and neglect that help explain why they evolved into spaces hostile to the lives of African American children. All but Del Paso Heights were originally all-white. As this chapter shows, Sacramento's long tradition of residential segregation dates to the early twentieth century, and acknowledging this history is key to understanding the current context of early childhood deaths in these neighborhoods. This section provides historical contexts for the seven neighborhood communities in which the BCLC is implementing its five strategies.

Oak Park

Established in 1887, Oak Park is Sacramento's oldest suburb. It offered working-class families an opportunity to own their home while living close to downtown Sacramento. It was like a city within a city, with its own thriving business district along Broadway and 35th Street. Few African American families resided in the district before World War II. However, the Second Great Migration, the redevelopment of the West End in downtown Sacramento, and housing discrimination in other neighborhoods that made them off-limits to African Americans brought many Black families to the area. Oak Park was one of the few areas where Blacks could easily purchase or rent property.

The steady flow of Black families into Oak Park in the 1950s and 1960s set off "white flight": the exodus of white residents and, in some cases, white-owned businesses, from an area becoming increasingly Black. By the late 1960s, Oak Park, which had one of the highest concentrations of African Americans in the city, had become Sacramento's epicenter of the "urban crisis"—a popular term used by the mainstream media and government to describe the plight of American cities struggling under the burdens of crime, unemployment, dilapidated housing, and so-called riots. Despite these signs of divestment and decline, Oak Park became the center of Black culture and activism. When the Black Panther Party established a chapter in Sacramento in 1968, it operated its headquarters on 35th Street.

Unfortunately, Oak Park never recovered from the economic fallout caused by the departure of homeowners and businesses. As the economic crisis of the 1970s worsened, so did Oak Park's fortunes. Despite the efforts of community activists and organizations like the Oak Park Project Area Committee to revitalize the area, the steering by the local real estate industry of African Americans and low-income residents into Oak Park and the concurrent practice of redlining on the part of banks and other financial institutions made such efforts nearly impossible. By 1980, public housing projects and a post office building had replaced the stretch of businesses that once stood along 35th Street.

The twenty-year period between 1980 and 2000 brought little substantial change to the area. This period could very well be described as Oak Park's nadir, as it housed high concentrations of poor, uneducated, unemployed, or underemployed residents seemingly untouched by the gains of the civil rights struggle. Parts of Oak Park have experienced a resurgence since about 2005, but this has come largely at the expense of its most vulnerable residents. Gentrification—the process of renovating and improving a house or district so that it conforms to middle-class taste—has certainly brought much-needed investment to the area. Restaurants and retail stories have returned to Oak Park's business district— now dubbed as the "Broadway Triangle." However, as property values and rents rise, many more low-income Oak Park residents will likely be pushed out.

Del Paso Heights

Del Paso Heights (DPH) is one of the oldest residential districts in the region north the American River. Located in the former Rancho Del Paso, DPH joined several new subdivisions that developed north of the American River in the 1940s and 1950s. Housing discrimination in other neighborhoods, combined with the availability of cheap land, attracted many African Americans to "the Heights." As in Oak Park, the Second Great Migration, along with the demolition of the West End, opened the floodgates for Blacks to move into DPH. As an unincorporated and largely rural district, DPH suffered from inadequate services and infrastructure before it was annexed by the city in 1959. Although annexation brought much-needed resources to the community, it did not bring dramatic improvements to the lives of residents. Making matters worse, DPH lacked a central business district that could have provided steady employment for area residents. Freeway construction in the 1960s bypassed business districts on Marysville, Rio Linda, and Del Paso Boulevards, further isolating DPH and creating unsustainable conditions for businesses to thrive. Few major shopping centers and a surplus of small liquor stores created a food desert for many residents. Redevelopment efforts in the 1970s, like those in Oak Park, failed to generate economic growth and reduce unemployment among residents. Though DPH is still a struggling community, it has experienced some improvement since about 2000. New housing developments such as Del Paso Nuevo and Renaissance provide moderate-income families the opportunity to purchase homes in the district. Community-based organizations such as the Roberts Family Development Center and the Mutual Assistance Network have worked tirelessly for decades to provide services to DPH families and children.

North Highlands

The North Highlands neighborhood was developed in response to the establishment of McClellan Air Force Base in 1936. That base, along with other defense-related industries, drew thousands of migrants to Sacramento during and after World War II. Eager to capitalize on this opportunity, local builders began to develop subdivisions near the base. Even though many African American servicemen worked at McClellan, the neighborhoods that made up North Highlands remained virtually all-white as they continued to exclude Black families. This was especially frustrating for Black employees at the base, forcing them to live in far-away areas like Del Paso Heights.

Despite having a high population density, North Highlands lacked adequate amenities and services primarily because of a lack of sufficient tax revenue: the area's largest employer, McClellan Air Force Base, was tax exempt because it was a military installation. Consequently, North Highlands was unable to maintain its parks, recreation programs, and fire services. Another factor that contributed to the area's decline was redlining.

A major blow to North Highlands came in 1995 when the federal government announced the closure of McClellan Air Force Base, along with 350 other bases throughout the nation. When the base officially shut down in 2001, it resulted in a loss of more than 11,000 people and over $500 million in payroll. Making matters worse, the Great Recession of 2008 had an especially devastating impact on the community. North Highlands, along with several other distressed neighborhoods in Sacramento with a significant Black concentration, experienced a disproportionate number of home foreclosures. Many homes in North Highlands were abandoned and remained vacant for years.

Meadowview

Meadowview was one of the many postwar suburbs in Sacramento County developed during the 1950s, providing affordable single-family homes to middle-class Sacramentans. It was located between Freeport Boulevard and 24th Street and from Florin Road to an area south of Meadowview. Up until the 1960s, South Sacramento remained overwhelmingly white. However, the influx of Black families moving into the suburb touched off a wave of white flight. Many whites did not welcome Black newcomers to their neighborhoods and believed in the myth that integrated neighborhoods lowered property values, created slums, and increased crime. The combination of Black in-migration and the problems created by overdevelopment and speculation only hastened the departure of white residents from the area.

White flight and the influx of low-income residents into Meadowview crippled the district's economic base. By 1990, many businesses operating in the area had left and been replaced by smaller businesses that employed fewer people and generated little revenue. Despite its problems, many Meadowview residents proved resilient throughout this period of transition and fought hard to bring needed resources to the area and to enhance its image. Meadowview has always had a proud history of civic engagement. After years of having almost no political representation at the municipal level, Meadowview acquired its own council seat in 1991 when the City Council redistricted the city. The following year, Sam Pannell was elected to represent the district. Pannell and, later, his wife Bonnie Pannell represented the district for more than twenty years.

Valley Hi

To the east of Meadowview lies the community of Valley Hi. Located west of Highway 99 and south of Mack Road, Valley Hi developed slowly. By 1975, it had around three thousand residents. Beginning in the 1980s, however, white flight gradually changed the face of the community, but like much of South Sacramento, it remained mostly white and middle-class. More than half of all homes were owner-occupied. Both Kaiser and Methodist Hospitals served the area and employed hundreds of people, Cosumnes River College enrolled more than ten thousand students, and the neighborhood featured several quality schools and recreational programs.

However, the narrative that predominated in the local media cast neighborhoods like Valley Hi and Meadowview as Sacramento's version of South Central Los Angeles. The Rodney King uprising in 1992 only heightened fear and anxiety. Much of the media coverage of Valley Hi during this period tended to present a simplistic view of a neighborhood in crisis, beset by high rates of crime, unemployment, and despair. Although Valley Hi did experience these problems, it also had a small yet thriving Black middle class. As with Meadowview, many African Americans were drawn to the suburb because it offered relatively affordable housing and decent amenities. Valley Hi, like many South Sacramento neighborhoods, took a serious hit during the Great Recession. Many Black residents took out subprime loans during the height of the housing boom only to see their monthly payments skyrocket beyond what they could afford to pay. In 2011, the *Bee* described Valley Hi as one of the epicenters of the foreclosure crisis, "converting scores of owners to tenants." This crisis had a devastating impact on Black homeownership and resulted in a major loss of wealth for African American families.

Fruitridge/Stockton

The Fruitridge-Stockton Boulevard district is located between 14th Street to the north and 47th Street to the south, and between Franklin Boulevard to the west and Stockton Boulevard to the east. It comprises several subdivisions built mostly between 1940 and 1960. This district developed during Sacramento's postwar housing boom and is one of several neighborhoods that expanded the southern boundaries of the Sacramento metropolitan area. A section of this area, known as the "Fruitridge Pocket," is unincorporated.

Originally, much of the area was farmland used primarily to grow wheat. With the demand for more housing, however, Sacramento area real estate developers such as John H. McMahon and Paul B. Ford developed what became known as the Fruitridge Shopping Center in the late 1950s. This popular shopping center served a growing population in South Sacramento. Although the FHA helped subsidize the expansion of the suburbs, it also contributed to residential segregation, requiring real estate developers to use race-restrictive covenants to keep out all African Americans. Taking its cue from the real estate industry, the FHA considered any neighborhood with African Americans as high risk and refused to provide mortgage insurance in these areas. Thus, many builders like McMahon and Ford made sure to keep their developments all-white. As a result, the Fruitridge-Stockton Boulevard district remained overwhelmingly white from 1950 to 1970.

White flight during the 1970s opened up homes in this area to Blacks. During the 1980s, large numbers of Southeast Asians and Latinos also moved into the district. Not coincidentally, as whites fled parts of the district, the neighborhood entered a period of decline. Many of the homes vacated by white families were rented to disadvantaged residents desperate for better housing options. However, a major turning point came in the 1980s with the introduction of crack cocaine to the neighborhood. The impact of this crisis cannot be underestimated. It led to rising addiction rates and unleashed a cycle of violence and turmoil that affects the neighborhood to this very day. The so-called War on Drugs upended the lives of many African American men and contributed to an increase in single-parent households, unemployment, and poverty. Making matters more complicated is the fact that the Fruitridge Pocket is unincorporated and has suffered from inadequate services for years.

Arden Arcade

Arden-Arcade is a census-designated place in Sacramento County northeast of downtown Sacramento. Its boundaries include Auburn Boulevard and Arcade Creek to the north, the American River (primarily) to the south, Ethan Way to the west, and Fair Oaks Boulevard to the east. Covering nearly nineteen square miles, it is a collection of dozens of neighborhoods with starkly different socio-economic makeup. Some neighborhoods like Arden Oaks and Arden Park Vista, Arden Park Estates, and Arden Hills Country Estates feature million-dollar homes and some of the most exclusive real estate in the Sacramento region, whereas others include a disproportionately high number of apartment buildings relative to other parts of the county.

The collection of neighborhoods that became known as Arden-Arcade had its origins during Sacramento's housing boom of the late 1940s. By 1960, Arden-Arcade had thousands of new single-family homes and bustling new shopping centers. Given Sacramento's racially segregated housing market, Arden-Arcade and most of its surrounding districts began their existence as lily-white suburbs. Since about 2010, Arden-Arcade has seen a rapid rise in residents who are living below the poverty line. Many immigrants and other residents—especially African Americans—who were priced out of other neighborhoods due to Sacramento's ongoing housing crisis have been attracted to

Arden Arcade because of its sheer volume of apartment units and one of the lowest rental rates in the area.

The killing of Stephon Clark in 2018 reinforced the nexus between residential segregation, poverty, crime, and policing in Sacramento County. Clark's neighborhood, Meadowview, had once been an all-white suburb that experienced an influx of African Americans in the late 1960s. Unlike some of the city's core neighborhoods, it had no race covenants barring African Americans. White flight and the influx of low-income residents into Meadowview crippled the district's economic base. According to the *Sacramento News and Review*, "That shift . . . is evidence of how a century of racist development policymaking yielded the environment that drives Sacramento policing to be at its twitchiest and most fearful in places like Meadowview where crime is relatively high and opportunity is relatively low" (Pyke 2018). Being born and raised under these circumstances significantly heightened the chances of Stephon Clark encountering law enforcement compared to the average white twenty-two-year-old in Curtis Park or McKinley Park.

As the fate of Stephon A. Clark reminds us, residential segregation has real consequences for African Americans in Sacramento. Sociologist Jesus Hernandez's research on residential segregation in Sacramento reveals that neighborhoods where African Americans and other non-whites are concentrated today experience the highest rates of poverty, unemployment, uninsured residents, and victims of predatory lending—these are the same neighborhoods where the BCLC has concentrated its efforts to combat high Black infant mortality (Hernandez 2009, 291–313). Indeed, in 2022 far too many poor and working-class people of color in the city are still trapped in the same historically redlined communities that deny homeowners the advantage of accruing equity and building wealth. Reckoning with the history of residential segregation and its continuing legacy will be absolutely critical to informing any discussion around remedies or reparations for victims of institutionalized racism in housing.

REFERENCES

Brilliant, Mark. 2010. *The Color of America Has Changed: How Racial Diversity Shaped Civil Rights Reform in California, 1941–1978*. New York: Oxford University Press.

Broussard, Albert S. 1993. *Black San Francisco: The Struggle for Racial Equality in the West, 1900–1954*. Lawrence: University Press of Kansas.

Cain, Leonard D. 1961. *Housing Discrimination in Metropolitan Sacramento*. Sacramento: Sacramento Committee for Fair Housing.

"California Secedes from the Union." 1964. *Sacramento Observer*.

Canson, Virna. 1984. "Waging the War on Poverty and Discrimination in California through the National Association for the Advancement of Colored People, 1953–

1974." Interview by Sarah Sharp, Regional Oral History Office, Government History Documentation Project, University of California, Berkeley.

Casstevens, Thomas W. 1967. *Politics, Housing, and Race Relations: California's Rumford Act and Proposition 14.* Berkeley: Institute of Governmental Studies, University of California.

"City Bans Discrimination in Mall Real Estate Plan." 1954. *Sacramento Union,* October 29.

"City Will Probe Housing Discrimination Charge." 1952. *Sacramento Bee,* January 4.

Colley, Nathaniel Sextus. 1984. Interview by Clarence Caesar, March 2, 1984. Black Oral Histories 1983/146. Sacramento Ethnic Communities Survey, Center for Sacramento History.

De Graaf, Lawrence B., Kevin Mulroy, and Quntard Taylor, eds. 2001. *Seeking El Dorado: African Americans in California.* Seattle: University of Washington Press.

Department of Savings and Loan. 1979. *Fair Lending Report 2,* no. 1. Sacramento.

Dingemans, D. 1979. "Redlining and Mortgage Lending in Sacramento." *Annals of the Association of American Geographers* 69, no. 2: 225–239.

"Dos Rios Homes Will Be Opened to Minority Groups." 1951. *Sacramento Bee,* December 26.

"Fair Housing Bill Following Argument." 1963. *Sacramento Union,* March 28.

"Fair Housing Committee Plans to Elect Officers." 1961. *Sacramento Bee,* April 26.

Flamming, Douglas. 2000. "Becoming Democrats: Liberal Politics and the African American Community in Los Angeles, 1930–1965." In *Seeking El Dorado,* edited by Lawrence B. De Graaf, Kevin Mulroy, and Quntard Taylor. Seattle: University of Washington Press.

"Groups Sue to Prevent Negro Ban in Housing." 1952. *Sacramento Bee,* February 2.

Hernandez, Jesus. 2009. "Redlining Revisited: Mortgage Lending Patterns in Sacramento, 1930–2004." *International Journal of Urban and Regional Research* 33, no. 2: 291–313.

Hirsch, Arnold R. 2000. "'Containment' on the Home Front: Race and Federal Housing Policy from the New Deal to the Cold War." *Journal of Urban History* 26, no. 2: 158–189.

Hirsch, Arnold R. 1992. "With or without Jim Crow: Black Residential Segregation in the United States." In *Urban Policy in Twentieth-Century America,* edited by Arnold R. Hirsch and Raymond A. Mohl. New Brunswick, NJ: Rutgers University Press.

Horne, Gerald. 1997. *Fire This Time: The Watts Uprising and the 1960s.* New York: Da Capo Press.

"Housing Bill Clears Committee." 1963. *Sacramento Observer,* March 28.

"Housing Bill Goes to the Assembly Floor." 1963. *Sacramento Bee,* March 28.

"Housing Heads Surrender on Racial Issue." 1952. *Sacramento Bee,* April 1.

Hudson, Lynn M. 2020. *West of Jim Crow: The Fight against California's Color Line.* Urbana: University of Illinois Press.

"Integration Policy Is Set in Sacramento Housing Projects." 1952. *Sacramento Bee,* January 31.

"Law Banning Realty Racial Laws Is Asked." 1954. *Sacramento Bee,* September 17.

Lee, K. W., and L. Lee, L. 1973. "Del Paso Heights: A City Apart." *Sacramento Union.*

Littlewood, S. 1960. "Tour Stresses Dilemmas of Minority Housing." *Sacramento Bee,* December 18.

Massey, Douglas S., and Nancy A. Denton. 1993. *American Apartheid: Segregation and the Making of the Underclass.* Cambridge, MA: Harvard University Press.

Mayer, William. 1953. "Sacramento's Housing Fight." *The Crisis,* January.

National Association for the Advancement of Colored People, Region I, Records, BANC MSS 78/180 c. 1952. Minutes of Meeting of Legal Committee, Western Region, National Association for the Advancement of Colored People. Bancroft Library, University of California, Berkeley.

National Association for the Advancement of Colored People, Region I, Records, BANC MSS 78/180 c. 1954. Constance Baker Motley to Franklin H. Williams. Bancroft Library, University of California, Berkeley.

National Association for the Advancement of Colored People, Region I, Records, BANC MSS 78/180 c. 1954. Freedom's Frontier: A Statement of the N.A.A.C.P. West Coast Region Committee. Bancroft Library, University of California, Berkeley.

National Association for the Advancement of Colored People, Region I, Records, BANC MSS 78/180 c. 1954. Proposed City Ordinance for the Prevention of Discrimination in Ownership, Use, and Occupancy of Real Estate in the City of Sacramento. Bancroft Library, University of California, Berkeley.

"N.A.A.C.P. Endorses Redevelopment as Council Acts." 1954. *Sacramento City Council Meeting Minutes*, October 28.

"NAACP Head Hits Housing, Hiring 'Evil.'" 1955. *Los Angeles Sentinel*, March 24.

NAACP West Coast Region. 1965. Report from Region I. National Association for the Advancement of Colored People West Coast Region I Papers, 1945–1977. Bancroft Library, University of California, Berkeley."

"N.A.A.C.P. West Coast Regional Reorganization Conference" 1951, National Association for the Advancement of Colored People, Region I, Records, BANC MSS 78/180 c, Bancroft Library, University of California, Berkeley

"Negroes on Coast Win Housing Case." 1958. *New York Times*, June 29.

"Oliver Ming Sues Real Estate Men for $5000." 1954. *Sacramento Outlook*, May 21.

Pyke, Alan. 2018. "Mapping Racism." *Sacramento News and Review*, April 5. https://www.newsreview.com/sacramento/content/mapping-racism/26077289/.

"Race Equality Body Stages Capitol Sit-In." 1963. *Sacramento Bee*, May 29.

"Rules out Biased Home Deals." 1958. *Chicago Defender*, July 5.

"Rumford Act's Aim Is Clear: To Block Discrimination." 1963. *Sacramento Bee*, December 23.

"Salvaging the Good." 1964. *Sacramento Observer*, November 12.

Somerville, John A. 1949. *Man of Color: An Autobiography. A Factual Report on the Status of the American Negro Today*. Los Angeles: L. L. Morrison.

"S.S.C. Prof Says Segregation in City Increases." 1961. *Sacramento Bee*, May 22.

"State Fair Housing Bill Is Passed." 1963. *Sacramento Observer*, June 21.

"Suit Charges Race Bias in Area Housing." 1954. *Sacramento Bee*, May 10.

Part 2
LEARNING

In "Part 2. Learning," Torry Winn, Patrice Hill, Quadir Chouteau, Kenneth Duncan and David Gonzalez highlight the ways in which healing is critical in education and youth development. The authors explore these questions: What is the connection between schooling and the well-being of Black children? What can history teach us about educating Black children? What community efforts and Black-led education initiatives offer solutions? What are the ways in which art, poetry, and creativity can be used to provide Black children opportunities to learn and teachers to instruct? How do we create spaces (in and out of school) for youth to grieve, reflect, and discuss social issues such as gun violence, police brutality, and anti-Blackness? Torry, Patrice, Quadir, Kenneth, and David provide examples from history and personal experiences to demonstrate how the BCLC is affecting the learning of Black youth. According to Julian Bond, "Violence is Black children going to school for 12 years and receiving 6 years' worth of education." Part 2 describes how the BCLC and Black educators are working to avoid educational violence by creating, designing, and building Black joy and honoring legacies within and beyond the walls of schools.

BLACK EDUCATION MATTERS

A Legacy of Educating Black Children
beyond the Walls of Public Schools

Lawrence "Torry" Winn

The struggle for quality education for Black children in the United States has been well documented. In *Brown v. the Board of Education of Topeka* (1954), the landmark U.S. Supreme Court case for public education, the Supreme Court overturned the practice of separate but equal in public schools permitted by *Plessy v. Ferguson* (1896). In its 1954 ruling, the Court stated that the separate but equal doctrine was to end with "deliberate speed." After the *Brown* decision, the courageous acts of the "Little Rock Nine," Ruby Bridges in New Orleans, and Medgar Evers in Mississippi made it possible for all students to attend K–12 public schools and colleges regardless of race or ethnicity. Although these legal decisions and heroic actions led to educational opportunities for some students, public schools have failed the vast majority of Black students. They have experienced harm, harassment, and mediocre teaching in school districts controlled by predominantly white school boards and educators (Fisher 2008; Rickford 2016; Sleeter 2001; Souto-Manning and Winn 2019).

In response, Black communities have demanded that public schools change their curricula, hire more Black teachers, and teach culturally relevant pedagogy (Ladson Billings, 1995). Since the 1960s, hundreds of Black education initiatives have been created to combat inequities in education. The sense of urgency to radically transform education is best expressed by Cheryl Ann Fisher, the co-founder of Shule Jumamose, an African-centered Saturday school for children in Sacramento: "We started Shule Jumamose because as parents and as Black people we are concerned about the education Black children are getting in public schools. Because it in no way re-enforces their well-being nor does it create a sense of pride" ("New Schools" 1971). In Sacramento, the Black Child Legacy Campaign (BCLC) and other educational programs/schools are heeding the call to "create a sense of pride," highlight Black excellence, exemplify unity, and advocate for Black children in and beyond the walls of schools.

In this chapter, I explore some of the current inequities affecting Black students and the many ways in which the Black community in Sacramento has responded to public schools' educational malpractice. Nearly all the research about Black families' educational experiences and histories centers on major metropolitan areas such as New York, Chicago, and Los Angeles. This chapter highlights Sacramento community efforts to provide Black excellence in education: a community college program (Oak Park School of Afro American Thought); a local Independent Black Institution (Shule Jumamose); two charter school organizations founded by Black leaders (St. HOPE Public Schools and Fortune Schools); a Children's Defense Fund (CDF) Freedom School (Roberts Family Development Center), and a community education board (the Black Parallel School Board). These initiatives created a foundation for the BCLC on which to promote Black pride and love beyond the walls of Sacramento County's public schools.

Say It Ain't So: Sacramento Schools Leads California in Suspensions

For decades, policy makers, scholars, and data analysts published reports and studies illustrating the gaps between Blacks and whites in wealth, health, education, and housing (Badger et al. 2018; Coates 2014; Cohen 2015; Desmond 2017). African Americans leaders, parents, and community members knew for years that Black and Brown students were being suspended at alarming rates. In 2014, President Barack Obama's administration released *Civil Rights Data Collection: Data Snapshot School Discipline*, a report detailing the racial disparities in suspension rates in public schools (U.S. Department of Education Office for Civil Rights 2014). The next year, Wisconsin's *Race to Equity Report* revealed that there were 3,198 school suspensions of Black students in Madison compared to 1,130 suspensions of white students; in addition, African American children were fifteen times more likely to be suspended than white children (Wisconsin Council on Children and Families 2013). These harms to Black students were highlighted in the 2016 *Civil Rights Data Collection: Data Snapshot School Discipline* prepared by the U.S. Department of Education Office for Civil Rights:

- Black children represent 18% of preschool enrollment, but 48% of preschool children receiving more than one out-of-school suspension; in comparison, white students represent 43% of preschool enrollment but 26% of preschool children receiving more than one out-of-school suspension.
- Black students are suspended and expelled at a rate three times greater than white students. On average, 5% of white students are suspended compared to 16% of Black students.
- Although boys receive more than two out of three suspensions Black girls were suspended at a higher rate than girls of every other ethnicity or race.

Black students and their families in public schools in Sacramento, the city that was named "America's most diverse city" by *Time Magazine* in 2002, were not spared from these inequities and injustices. Sacramento's progressive politics, diverse City Council and School Boards, and racially integrated schools proved unable to protect Black students from these racial inequities and racist policies. School districts in Sacramento County such as the Sacramento City Unified School District, Elk Grove School District, Twin Rivers Unified, and San Juan Unified had the highest number of suspensions for Black males in California (Wood, Harris, and Howard 2018). *Get Out! Black Male Suspensions in California Public Schools* (2018) revealed that Black males were 5.4 times more likely to be suspended in Sacramento County than the statewide average rate of suspensions. In 2016 and 2017, Sacramento City Unified School District had suspended 20.7 percent of its Black male students, leading all districts in the proportion of Black males who were suspended. Other key findings of *Get Out!* include the following:

- Eighteen Black males were suspended per day in Sacramento County public schools.
- Of the twenty school districts with the highest rates of suspension for Black males in California, four are in Sacramento County.
- Black males in early childhood education (kindergarten through third grade) are 9.9 times more likely to be suspended than their peers (statewide).

Black students are often over-policed, targeted, and profiled on and off school campuses. For example, in South Carolina an African American high school girl was dragged from her desk by a school resource officer (Winn 2020). In 2018, in Madison, a teacher grabbed the braids of an African American girl in middle school. The suspension data from these two reports, *Civil Rights Data Collection:*

Data Snapshot School Discipline and *Get Out! Black Male Suspensions in California Public Schools*, reflect the ongoing criminalization of Black students in PK–12 schools. However, although some describe schools as part of the prison pipeline, scholar-activists Erica Meiners and Damion Sojourner argue against this characterization because it fails to capture the complexities and the histories of the ways schools, communities, and other systems push students out of schools. (Meiners 2011; Sojoyrner 2016, Winn 2019).

Countering Public School Failure: Community Models of Black Education

Despite the failure of schools to educate Black students, Black communities have found ways to ensure that their children receive the skills and knowledge necessary for success. In *We Are an African People*, Rickford (2016, 39) provides a historical overview of the various Independent Black Institutions established to instill Black pride, Black love, Black culture, Black value, and Black excellence: "Black parents, children, and activists, sought educational dignity and the right to define themselves within and beyond the classroom." Similarly, Siddle Walker (1996, 141) highlights the success of Black teachers in the Casewell County Training School in North Carolina. Their goal was to develop relationships with students and their families, provide opportunities, and to ensure that every child reached "their highest potential."

Data show that Sacramento County public schools prevent Black children from reaching their highest potential. Most schools center and normalize whiteness in their teaching and curricula. The values and beliefs of Black folk are neither prioritized nor acknowledged (Sleeter 2001). Carl Pinkston, the secretary of the Black Parallel School Board, recalled that at one community meeting, a parent reported, "I go to school boards and I am given only two minutes to talk and I can't tell my story in two minutes of what is wrong with my kid . . . the people sit up there and don't respond to me and don't ask any question, I don't know if they are interested . . . and there is no one who follows up after I mention of why is my kid is being suspended and not getting a quality education" (https://blackparallelschoolboard.com/).

Thus, school districts in Sacramento County have failed both the Black child and the parent. In 1973 Chicago native Hakki Madhubuti (1973, 47) called for Black parents and community leaders to be institution builders: "If you know what we want people to become, then you can specify what they should experience from birth to adolescence and they will become it. But to do this one must control institutions and Black people don't control institutions."

In the next section, I provide brief descriptions of past and current Black-led initiatives and organizations that advocate for Black students to have access to quality education that is inclusive, not harmful, and culturally responsive. All these educational initiatives align with BCLC's goal of building supportive spaces for Black families and children to learn, grow, share, and experience joy. They all put community participation at the center of their work. Each organization and initiative collaborate with parents and local stakeholders to come up with educational goals that meet the needs of students and reflect best practices.

Oak Park School of Afro American Thought

During the 1960s, the Sacramento City College Black Student Union (BSU) became a powerful organization advocating for decolonizing education. BSU students were concerned about the lack of Black stories and experiences in traditional history classes. After negotiating with college president Sam Kipp, the BSU's proposal for a center focusing on Black life and education came to fruition (Barth 2015). In the summer of 1969, the Oak Park School of Afro American Thought was established to connect college students to the Black community of Oak Park. James Fisher and several Sacramento City College professors offered courses such as "Ghetto Economics (Consumer Problems)," "Black Drama," and "History 15" in the evenings to accommodate residents who were working during the day, parents, and those who were unable to pursue their degrees full-time. The Oak Park School of Afro American Thought lasted only a few years, but Black students' determination to create an educational experience that reflected their values, history, and realities had a lasting impact.

Shule Jumamose

Cheryl A. Fisher along with several Black nurses, Martha Reid and Bertha Gorman, cofounded Shule Jumamose—an African-centered Saturday school located in Oak Park (Fisher 2008). The school was operated by a group of African American parents led by Dr. James Fisher, to teach Black children their history and culture that were not taught in public schools. The teaching philosophy was based on Nguzu Saba or the seven principles of Kwanzaa: Umoja (unity); Kujichagulilia (self-determination); Ujima (collective work and responsibility); Ujimaa (cooperative economics), Nia (purpose); Kuumba (creativity); and Imani (faith). The school, part of a national network for Independent Black Institutions, hosted Sacramento's first Black film festival in 1970 and the first Kwanzaa ceremony in 1971 (Fisher 2008). Shule Jumamose became a beacon of community-engaged scholarship: local college students from California State University, Sacramento, and the University of California, Davis, taught courses, mentored youth, and volunteered at the school.

St. HOPE

After more than a decade of Sacramento schools failing to graduate Black students from high school, Kevin Johnson, who would later be the mayor of Sacramento from 2008 to 2016, founded St. HOPE Academy in 1989 to provide robust educational options for Black children and their families. It opened in a portable classroom at his alma mater, Sacramento High School, as an afterschool program serving schoolchildren and high school students in the local community. However, realizing that education alone would not change the futures of Black children and their families, St. HOPE soon adopted a holistic community development approach. With the 2003 opening of the 40 Acres Art and Cultural Center, a 25,000-square-foot mixed-use facility that included Underground Books, the Guild Theater, a café, and a barbershop, Oak Park became a destination for Black families. That same year, St. HOPE Public Schools was launched to provide a rigorous and quality urban pre-K–12 public education (sthope.org). St. HOPE Public Schools now include PS7 Elementary, PS7 Middle, Oak Park Prep, and Sacramento Charter High School. Most of the students at these schools are Black, and Sacramento Charter High School has the highest college-going rate for Black students in the state of California.

Fortune Schools

Dr. Rex Fortune, a school superintendent for twenty years, recognized the need for a more diverse teaching pipeline in science and mathematics (STEM) instruction. In 1989 he established the Fortune School of Education to prepare educators and train administrators to serve the most diverse school populations. Beginning in 2008, under the leadership of Margaret Fortune, Fortune Schools opened five public charter schools in Sacramento that are designed to close the opportunity gaps between white and African American children. Each of the five charter schools is named for a Black leader and offers a college-prep curriculum.

Roberts Family Development Center and Freedom Schools

The Roberts Family Development Center (RFDC) provides academic opportunities for more than 500 African American students and their families. Cofounded by Derrell and Tina Roberts in 2001, it is located in the Del Paso Heights community. It offers services at seven sites in under-resourced neighborhoods. Operating as an afterschool program and beyond the walls of the schools, RFDC aims to increase the life chances and educational options for African American students. It offers a "cradle to career pipeline" to support families by offering courses and trainings for both children and parents. In 2014, RFDC was selected to open a Children's Defense Fund (CDF) Freedom School. This six-week program, serving more than 700 students, helps participants avoid summer learning loss by focusing on literacy and culturally relevant interactive activities. Students read books written by African American authors and interact with Servant Leader Interns throughout the day.

Black Parallel School Board

In 2007, the Sacramento Area Black Caucus Education Committee held a community meeting to discuss a report highlighting low test scores for local African American students. Parents were frustrated not only by their children's scores but also by the lack of time (two minutes) to express their concerns at the Sacramento City Unified School District School Board meetings. In 2008, the Sacramento Black Parallel School Board (BPSB) was launched to work parallel to the Sacramento City Unified District Board of Education to monitor its activities and hold it accountable. The BPSB aims to ensure that Black students receive academic support to cultivate their educational growth. BPSB goals include the following:

- Create a twenty-first-century learning community with high graduation rates, high rates of transfers from community college to four-year colleges, and near-zero suspension and expulsions
- Train district staff in culturally responsive learning, restorative practices, and classroom management that focus on best-practice teaching strategies and Black learning styles
- Formulate a district intervention plan for improving Black academic achievement and fostering positive social and emotional development
- Decriminalize schools by supporting positive school environments
- Achieve a significant increase in the California State test scores for African-descended students in the district
- Make a realistic effort to have African-descended teachers make up 21 percent of the teaching force and an equitable increase in African-descended administration staff in the district with a 75 percent retention rate

- Create a positive learning environment for all Black students with special needs and temporary settings (such as housing).

The Path Forward to Educating Black Children beyond the Classroom

It is imperative to address educational challenges through the community engagement of diverse institutional and organizational stakeholders. Schools are not isolated from society but are intricately embedded inside communities and cities (Noguera 2003). To address what happens within the schoolhouse, it is important that researchers consider the larger ecosystem of a child's development (Bronfenbrenner 1979; Dance 2002; Watson 2012). This connects directly to the Black Child Legacy Campaign.

As do the educational efforts mentioned in the last section, BCLC centers Black culture, excellence, and success. Crystal Harding, a BCLC site leader, described BCLC as a space for Black folk to uplift one another and to discuss ways to reeducate and decolonize both the Black child and parent. It embodies the principles of Kwanza, which guide the offerings at Shule Jumamose. She added that the words "Black Child Legacy" in the organization's name and its promotion of Black life and success positively affect Black students, who do not see these images or examples in their schools. Harding's assessment of BCLC's role in education aligns with the words of Madhubuti in *From Plan to Planet: Life Studies: The Need for Afrikan Minds and Institutions* (1973, 33): "Nobody can instill black values except Black people. Our abilities to conceptualize and to act for our future depends on who has been feeding us our concepts."

As history has proven, public schools fail to educate the Black student because of a system that centers whiteness and devalues Blackness. Black-led educational programs and schools in the Sacramento Valley have sought various paths to instill Black values in Black children. The groundwork has been laid for the BCLC and its affiliates to "define themselves within and beyond the classroom" and become whom they believe their children to be.

REFERENCES

Badger, Emily, Claire Cain Miller, Adam Pearce, and Kevin Quealy. 2018. "Extensive Data Shows Punishing Reach of Racism for Black Boys." *New York Times*, March 19.
Barth, T. 2015. "Catalyst for Change." *Sac City Express*, February 6.
Bronfenbrenner, Urie, 1979. *The Ecology of Human Development*. Cambridge, MA: Harvard University Press.
Coates, Tehisi-Na. 2014. "The Case for Reparations." *The Atlantic*, May 21.

Cohen, Patricia. 2015. "Racial Wealth Gap Persists despite Degree, Study Says." *New York Times*, August 16.

Dance, Lory J. 2002. *Tough Fronts: The Impact of Street Culture on Schooling.* New York: Routledge.

Desmond, Matthew. 2017. "How Homeownership Became the Engine of American Inequality." *New York Times*, May 9.

Fisher, Maisha T. 2008. *Black Literate Lives: Historical and Contemporary Perspectives.* New York: Routledge.

Ladson-Billings, Gloria. 1995. "But That's Just Good Teaching! The Case for Culturally Relevant Pedagogy." *Theory into Practice* 34, no. 3, 159–165.

Madhubuti, Haki R. 1973. *From Plan to Planet: Life Studies: The Need for Afrikan Minds and Institutions.* Chicago: Third World Press.

Meiners, Erica R. 2011. "Ending the School-to-Prison Pipeline/Building Abolition Futures." *Urban Review* 43, no. 4: 547–565.

"New School Aims to Aid Black Youth." 1971. *Sacramento Bee*, June 23.

Noguera, Pedro. 2003. *City Schools and the American Dream.* New York: Teachers College Press.

Rickford, Russell. 2016. *We Are an African People: Independent Education, Black Power, and the Radical Imagination.* New York: Oxford University Press.

Siddle Walker, Vanessa. 1996. *Their Highest Potential: An African American School Community in the Segregated South.* Chapel Hill: University of North Carolina Press.

Sleeter, Christine. 2001. "Preparing Teachers for Culturally Diverse Schools: Research and the Overwhelming Presence of Whiteness." *Journal of Teacher Education* 52, no. 2: 94–106.

Sojoyner, Damien M. 2016. *First Strike: Educational Enclosures in Black Los Angeles.* Minneapolis: University of Minnesota Press.

Souto-Manning, Mariana, and Lawrence T. Winn. 2019. "Toward Shared Commitments for Teacher Education: Transformative Justice as an Ethical Imperative." *Theory into Practice* 58, no. 4: 308–317.

U.S. Department of Education Office for Civil Rights. 2014. *Civil Rights Data Collection: Data Snapshot School Discipline.* March. http://www2.ed.gov/about/offices/list/ocr/docs/crdc-discipline-snapshot.pdf.

Watson, Vajra. 2012. *Learning to Liberate: Community-Based Solutions to the Crisis in Urban Education.* New York: Routledge.

Winn, Maisha T. 2019. *Girl Time: Literacy, Justice, and the School-to-Prison Pipeline.* New York: Teachers College Press.

Winn, Maisha T. 2020. *Justice on Both Sides: Transforming Education through Restorative Justice.* Cambridge, MA: Harvard Education Press.

Wisconsin Council on Children and Families. 2013. *Race to Equity: A Baseline Report on the State of Racial Disparities in Dane County.* http://racetoequity.net/baseline-report-state-racial-disparities-dane-county/.

Wood, J. Luke, Frank Harris III, and Tyrone C. Howard. 2018. *Get Out! Black Male Suspensions in California Public Schools.* San Diego: Community College Equity Assessment Lab and the UCLA Black Male Institute.

POETRY AS PEDAGOGY

A Black Educator's Reflection

Patrice Hill

I struggle every day because I'm Black
I struggle every day because I stand out in society
I struggle every day because I talk different
I struggle every day because I dress different
I struggle every day because the place I come from
I struggle every day because I'm Black
       —SAYS student, in-class journal free-write

Something detrimental happens to Black children when the only history they are exposed to in school is their ancestors being battered and in bondage. As a teaching artist, it is my duty to intentionally integrate and blend art, social justice, history, hip-hop, and current events in a historical and present context to help make learning more engaging, student centered, exciting, and empowering.

One of the most consistent and powerful ways I engage with Black youth in Sacramento is through my work as director of Sacramento Area Youth Speaks (SAYS). Founded in 2008 at UC Davis, SAYS strives to change the world through education and empowerment. Building on a foundation of critical literacy and spoken word performance poetry, SAYS breaks the chains of underachievement by elevating the voices of young people and creating spaces for students to become authors of their own lives and agents of change. Through SAYS I have been given access to a wide array of schools throughout the Sacramento region. I have facilitated residencies in more than twenty-five schools in the region and worked with thousands of students. Black youth are experiencing life in a way they often do not get the opportunity to explain, but they do have something to say.

Before the Black Child Legacy Campaign was created, there were small and intentional movements designed to improve the health and well-being of Black children in Sacramento, such as SAYS. An overwhelming number of youth murders occurred across the city of Sacramento in 2016. These violent and unprecedented murders disproportionately were of Black children. Before we understood the technical term "third-party homicide," we knew that Black children were victims of violence and homicide at an alarming rate and that the aftermath and trauma from these homicides were a detriment to the livelihood of Black children in Sacramento. The Sacramento Office of Violence Prevention (directed by Khaalid Muttaqi at the time) put out an RFP for curbing youth violence in the city. The call was simple: *keep Black children alive*. SAYS applied for these funds, and Project HEAL was born.

After SAYS was granted these violence prevention funds, we met with the administration at Luther Burbank High School to plan how to use these funds to support Black children at the school site during the school day. Although there were generously funded academic and cultural interventions for Black males on campus, Black girls were consistently left out of targeted interventions aimed at improving academic outcomes and social emotional health. The school administrators recommended that the SAYS grant be directed to Black females, who were creating and perpetuating a culture of violence and hostility at the school. Fighting, arguing, and disputes over social media were just some of the destructive behaviors exhibited by Black girls that were not conducive to a positive learning environment for them.

Project HEAL (Healing/Health, Education, Activism and Leadership) is a credited, elective course on the high school level, which is delivered every day of the week in a cohort-style format. It exclusively and unapologetically addresses the experiences of Black students and other students of color who are disproportionately confronting oppressive social systems, including their schools. Project HEAL is geared toward students who are having challenges with finding culturally relevant and supportive systems of care within school and are experiencing difficulties translating their brilliance into academic success.[1] It is one of the small but critical pieces of a focused effort to empower and serve Black children within the classroom walls. I am honored to have a stake and a leg in this work.

> Maybe there's a youth posted near your block right now
> Having to make the choice of being broke and go to school or come up
> The only way they know how
> It may seem crazy, but poetry can save lives
> So, if spoken word can save soul then why don't more youth know
> They can make school their hustle and be like the rose that grows through the
>   concrete
> Like Tupac told you and me
> Every Black child deserves to have a legacy
>   —Patrice Hill, "Every Black Child Deserves to Have a Legacy"

In Black Sacramento, violence had become a normal occurrence in the life of the community; unfortunately, the accompanying trauma was also normal. Project HEAL began two years before the Black Child Legacy Campaign was initiated but aligns directly with the BCLC's mission and vision of creating safe and healing spaces for Black children to live and thrive in Sacramento. If spaces for Black children to thrive do not exist in the schools they attend, we must build them.

As an educator with and for Black children, I am most involved in the BCLC's targeted prevention effort, "Issue 4: Third-Party Homicides." The BCLC defines third-party homicides as the killing of a child by a person with or without malice aforethought, where the perpetrator is not the primary caregiver. I have shown up in classrooms with Black children the Monday after a Black child is murdered on the weekend, attempting to make sense of the loss of another innocent Black child's life and to hold space for the Black children left to mourn the child who looked like them. For Black children and youth practitioners in Sacramento, third-party homicide is an unfortunate recurring tragedy that plagues the Black Sacramento community.

The reality is that Black children are forced to internalize the fact that Sacramento streets are not safe for them to live in, walk, drive, and thrive. Sacramento streets are borderlands where Black children must grapple with the grief of the continuous killings in and through these green-and-white sign streets. SAYS created healing-centered spaces with culturally relevant and supportive adults who help youth process grief.

> The youth out here dying in the streets
> We trying to Advance Peace
> The youth searching for peace
> So some carry piece to maintain peace
> But the pain of Black child slain on the concrete
> Means no peace and the cycle repeats
> How long the is the cycle going to repeat
> How many more funerals to attend for you and me?
> Every Black child deserves to have a legacy!
> —Patrice Hill, "Every Black Child Deserves to Have a Legacy"

Art is always needed to transform the culture of a city. SAYS has been in consistent partnership with the BCLC since its inception, participating in a myriad of events centered around bringing voice to and empowerment of Black children's and communities' stories through a focused effort on the preservation of life, voice, and resiliency of Black children. As a Black educator facilitating spaces of healing through intensive writing workshops based on the principles of poetry and spoken word, I employ the same pedagogical tools used with students inside the classroom for the core constituents in various BCLC Community Incubator Lead spaces.

I have curated innovative workshops at the BCLC annual GLORY (Giving, Love to, Our, Rising Youth) Conference and multiple BCLC events such the Kings and Queens Rise, Juneteenth Community Celebrations, and many youth and community pop-ups. Most notably I created the Black Child Legacy Poetic Service Announcement, which is used as a culturally relevant literacy tool to elevate the mission, vision, and urgency of the BCLC on an artistic platform.[2] My poem titled "Every Black Child Deserves to Have a Legacy" is both an honest and compassionate reflection of the goals of BCLC and reflects my experience teaching in middle and high schools across Sacramento: Take these liquor stores out our hoods and give us, us free

> Even if all we have is this poetry
> Let it be enough to swim through this poverty
> Let it build legacies
> Let it empower Black children to be free
> Let is strengthen you and me to be here for these beautiful Black children to able to build legacies
> —Patrice Hill, "Every Black Child Deserves to Have a Legacy"

There must be a shared understanding that there is not one program or movement that will save all Black children. We must continue to work in partnership with one another to do all we can in our specific fields and using our specific expertise to save and empower Black children. How do we build legacies when freedom isn't free?

As an educator, I am often faced with the reality that most of the Black children I work with in K–12 public school systems in the greater Sacramento region often do not see themselves reflected positively in their curriculum. They are familiar with the familiar—slavery and some pieces of the civil rights movement. However, their knowledge is often limited. As a Black educator for Black children, I know how imperative it is that Black youth see themselves reflected consistently and courageously in the curriculum. There is an urgent need for Black youth to be exposed to the historic accomplishments, art, experiences, and achievements of Black folks, which they have contributed to in American life and culture.

Using poetry, spoken word, and hip-hop, I facilitate a classroom experience that ignites and inspires, motivates and transforms. As an educator and a community-based teaching artist, it is my honor, purpose, and duty to serve

Black youth. I do this most effectively by curating classroom experiences rooted in youth voice and social justice and developing a curriculum that is culturally relevant, responsive, and deeply engaging for Black children.

> My story is for those just like me
> My story is for young black boys who have been misled
> My story if for my younger brothers and sisters
> My story is for those looking for a place is this world
> I come from where you get or get got
> Where you run when you hear that gun pop
> Where more people are sent to prisons than schools
> These streets are cruel
> Us thugs and thots right?
> We are shot down on our way to work and on our way to school
> Why is it that a teacher would rather fail you than help you?
>
> —SAYS student, "My Story Is for . . ."

It is very difficult to fully describe everything that encompasses Project HEAL. No answer can give space to all the magic that is manifested in this transformative classroom space.

I walk into a classroom space where the curriculum surrenders to the stories, the plights, and profound pieces of the art, music, and history that have been left behind. There is healthy debate about concepts, movements, and people who have never made their way onto our students' history books. Multiple perspectives are presented of folks sacrificing their lives, leaving legacies and blueprints for us to continue the education and liberation fight. Some were wrong, but most were right. We discuss movements and deep writings describing life in the past and more recently.

In this classroom space we internalize the lives of artists and freedom fighters who together waged the war on injustice, deciphering their messages in the music, black codes, and genocide. In this classroom space we carve out intentional time to study what they have done and are doing to us; we analyze historical documents and the planned attempts to suppress us. We delve into documentaries, developing reflections of who we are and all we are meant to be.

These classroom walls sing a song of freedom, of sacrifice, of honor to the ones who risked their lives, primarily so Black youth could stay alive. Survive. Thrive.

> At this point in life
> I am angry, anxious, and confused
> Searching for what to become in life

At this point in life
I am exhausted, depressed and frustrated because
I've got this far in life and still don't know where life is taking me.

At this point in life, I'm struggling in all types of ways.
At this point in life, I struggle with working hard and trying hard.
At this point in life, I'm ready to finish school and go to college.
At this point in life, I'm ready for whatever comes my way.
Even though I'm going through some things.
I keep pushing.

—SAYS student, "What To Become"

I walk into a classroom space where there are no stories that do not involve pain. A display on a wall, titled "Rest in Power," gives visual representation to those who have been violently ripped away—youth murdered before they could graduate, youth of various hues who didn't get to finish high school. In this classroom we share the collective blues. In this classroom we know about red snow too. In this classroom space we remember all that these Sacramento streets have given and all that they take away. We repeat the names of our loved ones who have passed so their memories don't fade away. In this classroom space, the libations are poured onto the page. In this classroom, we learn what it means to say "Ase" (a Yorube word meaning "so be it").

In this classroom space we collectively confront fear and individually tackle the grief. In this classroom space we pick up our pens and let the pain speak. In this classroom space we look in the mirror and see our ancestors reflecting life through the students who choose to speak. Students eventually gain the courage to get past the fear and become confident to speak about their future and becoming all they dream they can confidently be.

I am a beautiful Black Queen
As though people don't see me as me
I keep pushing because
I know what I want to be
Head held high
No matter what the case may be
My Black is beautiful
Like a sunset in disguise
One day I will rise
Success is on my mind
And I will grind until it's time
If you're not on the same level, then stay behind

Hate is in the air
And it's an increase in Black crime
Martin Luther King Jr. would be out his mind
He fought for our freedom
And we're letting him down
We all need to come together
And make him proud.

—SAYS student, "My Story Is for . . ."

In this classroom space there is courage in the composition books; brilliance in the banter, word play, and the word of the day, some crying; and lots of laughter. In this classroom space there is no judgment, no fear. In this classroom space Black children are acknowledged and celebrated. In this classroom space we study Sojourner and Sista Souljah, Garvey and Rosa.

Using poetry and spoken word in the classroom is a transformational process. It essentially turns the classroom into a healing space where learning is reciprocal and both student and teacher are free to be our true authentic selves. It is a safe, student-centered space that is empowering, authentic, and free from judgment and from fear. It is a reflective classroom space, where we can learn about each other in a way that connects our differences and highlights how we are most alike.

In this classroom space, melanin radiates, and learning is experienced in a safe and sacred space. There are no wrong answers, Dear, and any truth you share will be protected here. No one will take your truth and make fun of you. In this classroom space, empathy resonates: we are more understanding humans because we choose to stand in truth.

In this classroom space, it is a must that we authentically partner with youth, because we know the youth only speak of truth: truly partnering with youth means there is no big me and no little you. In this classroom we are righteously equals, where the educator learns just as much from the students, always takes into consideration their points of view, and highly values their lived experiences as valuable classroom tools. Youth are encouraged to speak up and stand in their truth, nor are they belittled when they have an alternative point of view. In this classroom space we partner with youth because they can help develop the curriculum we use. Youth can build measurements to double study (examining the curriculum and not just taking lessons at face value, especially when it is Eurocentric and inaccurate) to make sure what they are learning is the truth. Youth are given opportunities to develop their agency and public speaking skills, which they can use beyond the classroom.

Youth are motivated to enter youth poetry slams and be a part of the Brave New Voices International Poetry Festival and Slam, which changes locations every year. In Sacramento, young people throughout the region compete in "Slam Season" and the winners comprise the SAYS Slam team. These students compete at Brave New Voices and also serve as ambassadors of youth voice throughout the city.

Youth agency is elevated when they are taken to City Council meetings not just to observe but also to sign up for public comment and get their three minutes to speak, authentically reflecting on political matters that affect their education and communities. The youth can tell us all they need; it is up to us heed the words they speak.

In this classroom there are prestigious poetry program pipelines. A student could be crowned the Sacramento Youth Poet Laureate, which could lead them to their being chosen as the next National Youth Poet Laureate of the United States and have the opportunity to travel and perform their poetry at prestigious universities and important events in other states; they could perform on the National Mall and even in front of people who paid to hear them speak in poetry.

In this classroom the power is in the voice of the youth, and it is our duty to see it through. Youth voice is one of the most valuable tools we have in transforming education. Young people have so much to say, but they are often limited in the spaces where they can truly be their authentic selves without censorship. Creating environments where youth voice is embraced and not feared allows young people to have a critical stake in their future. It allows for honest feedback about how young people are receiving and navigating their education. When young people become the authors of their own lives, they become agents of change.

In my time as an educator, I witnessed many schools and systems become disengaged from youth voice, especially when it leads to youth developing personal agency that empowers them to speak their truth regarding their education. Sometimes the truth is too painful for schools to accept. When youth begin to question the value and the authenticity of their education, it further illuminates the inequities that plague our schools for Black children. Youth voice is all good until it puts young people in a position to advocate for themselves, to call out and name systems of harm within our educational system. Youth voice is great until young people are organizing school walkouts to address discriminatory school policies. Youth voice is powerful until youth are organizing and leading citywide protests, where hundreds of young people collectively march to the State Capital during the school day to speak out against injustice. Youth voice is amazing until youth are agents of change at their schools, debating history lessons with teachers and fighting against oppressions in tangible ways that directly confront oppressive education and community systems that harm and prohibit youth from living their best lives and accessing the resources needed to do so.

We need to be honest about the way we want youth voice to look: it cannot always be pretty. Youth voice reflects reality. Youth voice is purposeful and can be painful for false prophets. Youth voice calls for an honest appreciation of the good and the bad that the youth are experiencing. Constructive criticism can be hard to hear when you do not really want to listen. Youth voice is youth honesty, but do schools honestly want to hear what our children need to heal? Youth voice is the testament of what we are doing wrong with our youth, revealed. Youth voice exposes education, many schools aren't ready for that expose.

When we truly listen to young people, we are provided with brilliance and bravery. When we truly listen to young people, we are offered tangible solutions to complex problems. If we are brave enough to listen to youth, we receive critical and honest narrative about what they need to succeed and thrive. Don't we all want our young people to do more than survive?

> They don't care if my students get high at school
> Long as they get by at school
> Get by institutionalized racism and intergenerational oppressions systems
>   that keep
> Prison pipelines thriving and standardized test categorizing
> Even if all we have is this poetry
> Let it be enough to swim through this poverty
> Probably there's a youth posted near your block right now
> Having to make the choice of being broke and go to school
> Or come up the only way they know how
> It may seem crazy, but spoken word can saves souls
>   —Patrice Hill, "Every Black Child Deserves to Have a Legacy"

In this classroom space there is *Ago* and there is *Ame*; we usually begin our day with call-and-response.[3] Then we write in our empowerment journals and let the resistance spill on the page. We acknowledge that some of us live with the grief of losing a loved one every day.

The circle is a cipher (see figure 5.1).[4] There are no rooms for rows because our brilliance grows in a circular motion just like a rose. Straight from the deepest part of the dirtiest concrete, we come to push through barriers and be everything they said we couldn't be. In this classroom, we come to heal and build all

FIGURE 5.1.

that was stripped from us. We cool and we hustle school, just like the poets and wordsmiths before us. In this classroom poetry, spoken word, knowledge, and hip-hop define us.

In this classroom we engage in courageous conversation, facilitate diplomatic debates, resuscitate righteous rigor in a safe and creative space. In this classroom the standard is the self, and our testimonies tell on themselves: we are aiming to reach the fullest potential of our selves.

> Why we gotta scream to be heard?
> Why we gotta die to be recognized for being alive?
> Are our screams like triggers
> That spring you into action?
> Why we gotta die?
> Oh I'm sorry, did I interrupt your dinner?
> Did I interrupt your polite conversation about the weather?
> Oh excuse me!
> Was I too loud; did I shock you into existence are you woke now?
> Do you see me?
> Do you see me wounds or shall I paint a clearer picture?

Death don't get no clearer.
Was the pain not evident in my voice?
Are your butts at the edge of your seats now
Are you learning forward, inching closer?
Are you drawn to my sorrow?
Are you drawn to my pain?

—SAYS alumnus, "Are You Woke Now?"

In this classroom space we are shown the victories and changed trajectories made possible by higher education degrees. In this classroom we evaluate our transcripts so we can know our A through Gs. In this classroom space we have access to college campuses and can more clearly envision our academic journeys.

This work is more than a passion: it is the true *pedagogy of my life*. There is profound purpose in an intimate life calling to be a vessel to serve. Poetry has the power to transform spaces into those where we are free to speak our truth, free to be who we are, free to be fearless, free to grow, free to learn, and free to change. In those spaces, we are encouraged to become our ancestors' wildest dreams, to speak our truths, and to document the world as we see it.

I have had the opportunity to facilitate spaces where I am able to witness young people blossom into bearers of truth. They are fearlessly writing for their lives: writing to heal, writing to live, writing to win, writing to see a word more beautiful than the injustices we see, writing to be, and writing to believe that there is something bigger and better than what these schools tell our children they can be.

Every day I go to school with the world on my shoulders
Thinking of what complications these teachers have in order
You do your work on a daily
That still isn't enough
I think these teachers be playing me, purposely making it rough!
The Black skin on my body and the strong power in my heart
I honestly think that's where all my complications start
They see me trying as hard as I can
But yet all the white kids got all the A's in hand
All my brothers and sistas going through the same things
Don't give up, they needs to use us on them TV screens.

—SAYS student, "These Teachers"

There are too many young people who have not yet received a chance to become the author of their own life, to have the opportunity to tell their story in their own words. These youth have been silenced by schools and systems that refuse to recognize their brilliance. They are marginalized by the confines of institutionalized racism and never get an authentic chance to speak their mind; Youth who have experienced more than a lifetime worth of violence must secretly swallow their silence.

Poetry has the power to free us, to push us beyond the confinements of the classroom. Social justice arts education is an essential component of producing liberatory classrooms where learning is alive and the curriculum both speaks directly to the students' lives and liberates their minds. When classrooms become sanctuaries of scared spaces to speak from the soul, we all grow, we all heal, we all feel. We become more in touch with our humanity, and isn't that what we want our children to see?

I encourage my students to never stop writing. I tell them to confidently speak their truth—to say something, to stand firm in their beliefs, to speak up even when it is unpopular and you are afraid. I want Black youth in Sacramento to become empowered authors of their own lives, capable of determining their future, capable of telling their stories, capable of teaching the next generation how to use their voice. The youth are speaking: Are you listening?

In this classroom we are the words we speak, the limited food options we must eat, the trauma we live through, the healing we seek. In this classroom poverty is protagonist and poetry is pedagogy. In this classroom there is freedom in the pen, and we can always begin again. In this classroom there is a celebration of life and freedom to write. In this classroom we embody our right to write—our write to life.

> If poetry can save lives, then
> Why don't more youth know
> They can put down nines and pick up poetry lines
> Attend poetry night or the open mic
> And eventually
> Learn how to love to write
> Articulate their faith
> We done living in vain
> Be the rose that grows straight through the concrete
> Like our ancestors fought for you and me
> Every Black child deserves to have a legacy
>> —Patrice Hill, "Every Black Child Deserves to Have a Legacy"

NOTES

1. Teachers and school counselors identify and recommend students for the intervention course which is a year-long elective course. The students stay together for the entire

year and take the course together. Project HEAL was so successful with African American females that in subsequent years it expanded to include males.

2. This is a city-wide campaign that elevated spoken word artists discussing topics of youth violence, joy, and justice.

3. *Ago* is a West African word from Ghana that means "to pay attention or listen." It is a call for attention. *Ame* is a response to Ago. It means, "You have my attention."

4. The cypher (or cipher) has deep, long-standing cultural roots in hip hop culture where people stand together in a circle and share their artistic expression.

BLACK IN SCHOOL

Youth Reflection

Quadir Chouteau

I'm from South Sacramento. In 2017, my neighborhood was one of the murder capitals of California. Problem solving was second nature for kids from my area because you could be in a life-threatening situation. Losing friends, siblings, and relatives in the midst of street activity changed my outlook on life. While some people at my high school were focused on their GPAs, I was preoccupied with RIP t-shirts and funerals. Amidst atrocities, I excelled in school. Along the way, I advocated for a classroom that would allow us to heal.

It was difficult to focus on school when I was worried about loved ones. I knew I was not alone. Luther Burbank High School is located in the middle of active gang neighborhoods. Seeing violence, hearing police sirens, smelling marijuana while walking down the street, and carrying caskets are phenomena that shouldn't be part of our everyday lives. So, if death surrounds us, how do we deal with our trauma?

The answer is an elective class called Project HEAL, sponsored by the UC Davis SAYS program. Project HEAL stands for Health, Education, Activism, and Leadership. It changed my academic trajectory. In this course we discussed street violence and how to make "school my hustle." Moreover, the community-based educators who taught the class were from the same areas as we were. They connected the curriculum to our reality. The ability to lead a group of young men in the same predicament as me to a program they have never heard of before was unheard of by freshman. As my first year in high school progressed, I saw my friends' lives change. With SAYS, we took trips within and beyond Sacramento and it opened our eyes to a world we were not accustomed to. I was able to see new cities across California and throughout the country, and make connections with other youth. It was life-changing.

As a result, I found an oasis inside my high school that allowed me to soar. In my Project HEAL classroom, I could focus on my wellness and process my grief while still engaging in my international baccalaureate courses. My grades increased and I started to see my future—a future where I can further my skills as a problem solver in college.

> We have a powerful potential
> in our youth.
>
> —Mary McLeod Bethune, "Last Will & Testament"

DOING THE REAL WORK

Community Reflection

Kenneth Duncan Jr.

I am a Bay Area/Oakland native. I attended Meritt College and Laney College, both community colleges, in Oakland. I then received a basketball scholarship and transferred to Wilberforce University, an historically Black college/university (HBCU) in Ohio where I received my bachelor's degree in psychology.

I have a passion for helping youth become the best versions of themselves, even if no one else sees them in a positive light. After college I began working in the nonprofit world where my love and passion grew for mentoring and coaching our Black youth. In 2012, I became a program director for the Boys and Girls Clubs in Seavey Circle/New Helvetia public housing in Sacramento's Upper Land Park and continue to support and mentor the youth I worked with then. I have had the blessing of mentoring youth from elementary school to their early years of college and being able to help them enroll in HBCUs. One of the young people I mentored since the fifth grade is now a freshman at Grambling University.

In Sacramento, I have had the pleasure and grace to serve on both sides of the river, something rarely done in this work. I first served as the lead staff member of a Community Incubator Lead (CIL) in Oak Park and am currently the lead CIL in Del Paso Heights. Through the BCLC, we have been able to reach youth who are system-impacted (children in child welfare and/or criminal justice system) and work with youth who are experiencing incarceration through programs such as Kings and Queens Rise, a basketball league for which I am currently the commissioner. I also cofounded a mentoring group called Black Boys Build (BBB). In this article, I focus on my impact and day-to-day interaction with "at-promise youth" (Mireles-Rios et. al 2020; Watson, 2012) and on the importance of trust and relationships in communities we serve.

Crisis response and intervention are huge parts of this work. Our goal is to help those who have suffered traumatic situations to feel somewhat whole again. If a child loses a parent or a mother loses a child, we try to provide whatever we can to begin the healing and to connect families to housing or even support them to make the rent during hard times. We know that the pain does not go away soon (if ever), but we try and help ease that pain in the most difficult times.

Kings and Queens Rise

I have the honor of serving as co-commissioner of the Kings and Queens Rise Basketball league for the past two years. The league was created after the death of Stephon Clark, who was killed in his grandmother's back yard by the Sacramento police. It targets youth who normally do not have the opportunity to play on their school's basketball team. This league reaches more than 600 youth across the city of Sacramento each season, giving them an opportunity to play organized, competitive basketball and meet youth from different communities.

Each neighborhood served by the BCLC—Meadowview, North Highlands, Arden Arcade, Del Paso Heights/North Sacramento, Oak Park, Fruitridge/Stockton, and Valley Hi—plus New Helvetia/Seavey Circle are in the league. I was the head coach for New Helvetia/Seavey Circle and we won the championship at the Golden 1 Center, home of the Sacramento Kings. This was an amazing experience for our youth and for me, especially because I had been working for more than seven years with some of the team members. Some of our youth had never been to a Kings game, let alone been invited to play a game on the Kings' home court.

Black Boys Build

Black Boys Build is a support group for young men desiring community, mentorship, training, and guidance as they navigate through life. It provides a safe and nurturing environment for young men who may be involved in at-risk spaces, including probation, gang activity, or simply navigating reality as a young man of color. This group is facilitated primarily for Oak Park and Del Paso Heights youth but is open to young men throughout the city. We hold group sessions for twenty-five to thirty youth to encourage dialogue and healthy discussion. The young men learn and discuss topics concerning personal development, emotional management, relational equity, and more. Participants occasionally receive incentives for continuing to participate in sessions and recruiting others to attend with them. We look forward to growing with this group and to seeing how the young men will develop.

This work is my calling, not just my job. Every day, the young people teach me about life, persistence, and resistance. These skills are fundamental in sports, and are essential aspects of holistic youth development.

REFERENCES

Mireles-Rios, Rebeca, Victor M. Rios, Trevor Auldridge-Reveles, Marilyn Monroy, and Isaac Castro. 2020. "I Was Pushed out of School: Social and Emotional Approaches to a Youth Promotion Program." *Journal of Leadership, Equity, and Research* 6 no. 1: 1–21.

Watson, Vajra. 2012. *Learning to Liberate: Community-Based Solutions to the Crisis in Urban Education*. New York: Routledge.

HONORING THE LEGACY

Advocacy through Art

David Blanco Gonzalez and the Youth Participatory
Action Research Team

Legacy exists at the sacred intersection of life and death. Young people in Sacramento yearn for a way to memorialize their peers who passed away and so advocate for and honor Black life. In partnership, a local artist David Gonzalez and young people from the Mutual Assistance Network of the Arden Arcade Community Incubator Lead (CIL) for the Black Child Legacy Campaign developed a participatory action research project to elevate and honor the life of a child or young person killed in Sacramento County. The team became the Youth Voice Advocacy project and gives all the credit to the youth and the families involved who bravely shared their stories and who lead their neighborhoods to continued greatness every day.

Participatory Action Research Project

The Youth Voice Advocacy project gathered young people from all seven BCLC neighborhoods to talk about third-party homicide and the violence they witnessed in their communities. The youth are so often removed from conversations about how to combat violence, and yet they are often the closest to the pain when a young person's life has been taken. Throughout the meetings, they shared personal stories of their family members, friends, and peers falling victim to violence. The families of the victims were invited to meet with their neighborhood's youth and share their stories of how violence had affected them. Each neighborhood group then chose one victim to lift up through art who would represent their neighborhood.

David Gonzalez was commissioned to sit in on these meetings and create portraits of each of the victims chosen by the youth. He attended the meetings to hear the words and stories of the young people and families and to talk about his process of using art as a tool for healing. He used these conversations and stories as the foundation for his portraits, literally inscribing each blank canvas with the words and phrases shared by each neighborhood. David completed eight portraits, four of which are shown in figures 8.1–8.4. They were unveiled at a private showing for the families of the loved ones lost at the Sol Collective Arts and Cultural Center in Sacramento in 2018.

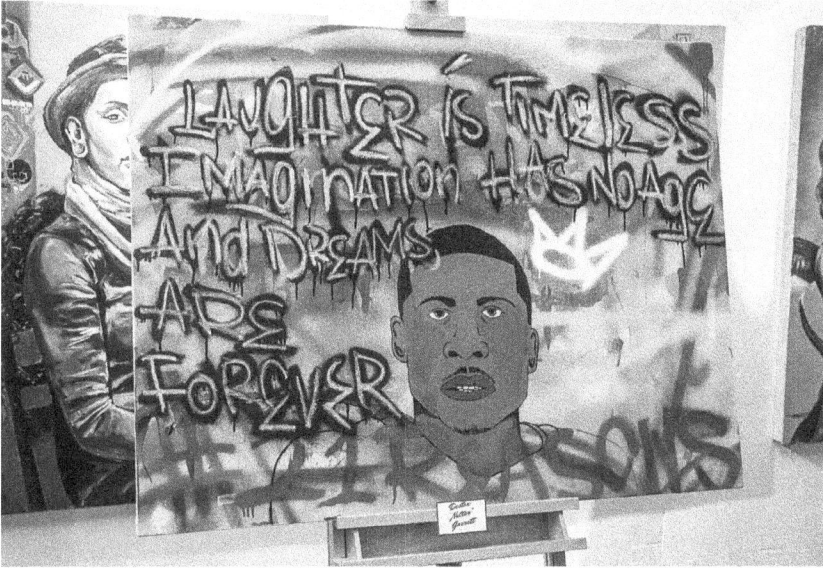

FIGURE 8.1.   Photographer: Terence Duffy (terenceduffy.com)

FIGURE 8.2. Photographer: Terence Duffy (terenceduffy.com)

FIGURE 8.3. Photographer: Terence Duffy (terenceduffy.com)

FIGURE 8.4. Photographer: Terence Duffy (terenceduffy.com)

REST IN POWER

Adrienne Ludd, North Highlands

Azalya Anderson, Valley Hi

De'Sean Rowe-Manns, Arden Arcade

Deston "Nutter" Garrett, Oak Park

Jacob Green, North Highlands

Jaulon "JJ" Clavo, Del Paso Heights

Stephon A. Clark, Meadowview

Timothy Jeter, Fruitridge-Stockton

Part 3
LEADERSHIP

We move from "Learning" to "Leadership" in this part. Who we are shapes how we lead, and Kindra Montgomery-Block and Ijeoma Ononuju demonstrate that personal transformations shape our experiences with and of community. In chapter 9, Kindra calls in some of the elders who inspired the work in Sacramento—naming Reverend Janet Wolf of the Children's Defense Fund—and others who guided a "common narrative around our collective goals." Subsequently, Ijeoma takes us to into the intricacies of community-based leadership and the importance of having a "license to operate." This part closes with an examination of the leaders who demanded economic accountability after the police killing of Stephon A. Clark. This murder "ignited a flame of unrest in the city of Sacramento" that prompted the creation of Build.Black. Building on the work of the Black Child Legacy Campaign, Build.Black. is a powerful economic development collaboration working throughout the city.

PATTERNS OF POSSIBILITY

Lessons Learned

Kindra F. Montgomery-Block

In 2018 and 2019, for the thirty months before the COVID-19 quarantine of 2020, there was not a single juvenile gun homicide in the city of Sacramento. Through a combination of collective impact strategies, coordinated program alignment, narrative change, deep OG neighborhood partnerships, funding, and faith, the Black Child Legacy Campaign (BCLC) seemed to have stopped gun violence. In this chapter I detail the connection and importance of the prophetic messages that facilitated BCLC's formation and early efforts, thereby advancing change and building a common narrative around our collective goals.

> I am held accountable by a community of folks for whom this is frontline stuff.
>
> —Rev. Dr. Janet Wolf, Children's Defense Fund

The Rev. Janet Wolf, director of the Children's Defense Fund Haley Farm and Nonviolent Organizing, is a God-given force for justice and action. She is a national luminary among prophetic, social justice theology and seminary students, organizers, preachers, gangsters, and community members. Her guidance is one of the main reasons for the early success of the BCLC.

For three consecutive years (2016–2018), BCLC leaders visited Haley Farm where the annual Proctor Institute was held on the third week in July. The Proctor Institute (named after the civil rights leader Samuel DeWitt Proctor) is a week-long conference held on a huge estate once owned by Alex Haley; it features rolling green hills, ponds, creeks, log cabins, a modern Noah's Ark, and a library named after Langston Hughes. It is a very special place. Attendees include seminary students, pastors and preachers, entire congregations, ex-convicts, law enforcement personnel, community organizers, public health officials, politicians, attorneys, civil rights leaders, teachers, professors, and young people of all ages. For many attendees, this is a spiritually fulfilling experience that makes them smarter and connects them to justice work, history, activism, collaboration, and political strategy. Early in the work of the BCLC, its leaders sat with Rev. Wolf and had cherished, encouraging, strategy conversations with her in the Ark at Proctor. She encouraged BCLC leaders to focus on the ten "patterns of possibility":

1. Figure out ways to listen with no sense of power. Go to where people are and listen. Listen to youth!
2. Compare your listening with data. Data only tells part of the story. It misses some of the harsher places and crises that people are going through.
3. If we don't listen, then we jump into solutions that don't work.
4. There are deep theological justifiers for so many of the systems that sabotage young Black folks. We need to redefine theological education.
5. If you believe that every child carries the mark of the Divine, then it is really hard to consign them to a cage in the juvenile justice system or not give them health care or adequate housing.
6. Nonviolent organizing—not movement building, but organizing—is slow and relational.
7. Primary voices matter. Dig deeper roots. Collaboration is important.
8. Be unapologetic for focusing on Black children. Whether you are standing in the street listening to stories or reading the newspaper, there is no question that Black people are the death-bound subject (JanMohamed 2005). If we can liberate, engage, and transform these death-dealing systems, it will benefit everyone.
9. End the cradle-to-prison pipeline.
10. You have the right to be in the room with people who have power.

The Proctor Institute and the patterns of possibility with which we wrestled played a large role in determining the early direction of the BCLC. Returning from the 2016 institute with a transformed commitment to BCLC's work, we decided to re-create a similar conference experience for BCLC stakeholders in Sacramento. We called our conference G.L.O.R.Y. (Giving Love to Our Rising Youth), and it was held for three consecutive years at the South Sacramento Christian Center in Valley Hi. In its first year, we invited the Rev. Michael Brandon McCormack to present the keynote address. A prophetic young Black Baptist pastor and faculty member in the Pan African Studies Department at the

University of Louisville, McCormack addressed the more than one hundred attendees, motivating us with these five precepts:

1. *Build faith*. Prophetic ministry is connected to the need to speak truth to power, and life to the powerless. Speak out against policies and practices that marginalize vulnerable populations.
2. *Connect trusted messengers*. There is a need to show and bring life to places where people are suffering.
3. *Undo intergenerational cycles of suffering and black trauma*. Black women carry an undealt with burden in communal violence and healing. It is essential to invest in and focus on Black women.
4. *Show up*. Don't just send resources. You have to be in the places in which children are suffering. You have to see and feel the sorrow.
5. *Stretch yourself*. When you are dealing with communities of color that have been on the receiving end of violence and pain, it is imperative to connect with the spiritual to have the strength and power to heal your community.

Through McCormack's powerful, prophetic message, BCLC leaders were able to build strength in our partnerships, fellowship with our community, and authenticity in our approach. We built commonality in our struggles and used the narrative "tail winds" of the current movement for Black lives to create community change.

The first death-bound youth to die of gun violence after the establishment of the BCLC was killed in June 2016. It was a hot Friday afternoon. BCLC leaders received a call from Chet Hewitt, CEO of the Sierra Health Foundation. A call from Chet on a Friday afternoon is never a good call. Chet asked, "Have you talked to Greg?"

"Nope, why what's up?"

"Give Greg a call; something is going on. A kid has been shot, and the whole school is up at the UC Davis Med Center. Two hundred Sac High kids have been there for two nights and days."

We jumped on a call with Greg King, CEO of Always Knocking, Inc., an innovative social rehabilitation program serving at-risk and incarcerated youth in the Sacramento area and the community OG first responder to local youth violence. King confirmed that a young Black Sac High School student had been shot, and the UCD medical staff were saying that he was not expected to pull through. The emergency department was full of Sac High students standing vigil; most of them had not eaten or slept since the news of the shooting. Hospital staff requested help clearing the youth out of the waiting room, but the situation was tense. Greg asked if we could order pizzas for the students and volunteers and make space for fellowship in a small outdoor quad off the emergency department waiting room. That, he said, would help deescalate the situation and provide a respite for students dealing with a traumatic situation.

I will never will forget the scene at the hospital when we arrived. There were teenagers everywhere—sleeping under tables, on planter boxes and chairs, and in stairwells. It was a frightening and sad mess. We also saw the victim's mother for the first time. She was outside the hospital, obviously distraught, smoking a cigarette, and being consoled. The BCLC volunteer team ordered the pizzas and, with the help of a few adults, were able to take the students outdoors. We could see, hear, and feel the group's mood change. As the pizza line started to get shorter, Greg walked up to us and asked, "You see that table way over there?"

We all looked up at the young men who sat slouched, "Heads up, 7up"-style, around the table. Their faces were not visible because their hoodies were drawn so tightly around their heads. It was too hot to have their hoodies up: something was wrong. When young people experience the tragic gun death of a peer, you can see in their faces that their world has become a dark place. Greg proceeded to tell us, "Those kids at that table are not hungry. They ain't talking; they are hurting. They know exactly what happened; they are losing their brother and they know it. I am going to go love on them." And he walked in their direction.

Greg King is good at listening, the same kind of "listening without power" that Rev. Wolf speaks about. We did not personally meet with or talk directly to those young men, but we did listen. The events of that day shook all of us deeply. The young Sac High student did succumb to his injuries. But that is not the end of this story because that young man's life and legacy live on through his mother, who has become one of the most beloved BCLC advocates and a Community Intervention Specialist trained to provide crisis response and violence reduction strategies to help other gun violence victims in her community. Her leadership has been instrumental to the Oak Park and Fruitridge/Stockton BCLC teams. Her healing approach comes from her ability to provide servant leadership, which focuses on the well-being of those being served and follows Rev. McCormack's call to *stretch yourself.*

This event was a pivotal moment for the BCLC. We knew we had to change the culture of gun violence crisis responses if we were to be a whole-family system of care. Dismantling death-bound systems was not going to be easy and could only be achieved through an ecological, upstream approach to violence disruption. Failure to prevent the loss of of a child's life is unforgivable, and in that moment, in the quad at the UCD Med Center, we could hear Reverend Wolf's voice: "Listen to the youth!"

We *did* listen to the youth and the faith-based leaders who provided a vision for BCLC. But this was not just listening according to the English usage of the word, meaning to give one's attention to sound. Instead, BCLC listening comes from the Spanish verb, *escuchar*, which means to listen with your heart. We doubled down on "heart listening" and purposefully built youth–adult partnerships. Sierra Health Foundation's leadership made Youth Participatory Action Research (YPAR) a grant priority, with youth participants receiving stipends; in addition, Community Incubator Leads (CILs) received annual funding, and the programs it supported were regularly assessed to ensure they aligned with BCLC priorities. Quarterly, BCLC youth and adult met at Profound Purpose Institutes (PPIs) for professional development training and focus group work. BCLC's CIL leaders became very familiar with the annual Sacramento County Annual Child Death Data Reports and were able to combine secondary health equity data gathered by BCLC with YPAR primary data to develop specific strategies to lift neighborhoods by prioritizing youth voice and engagement. For example, the YPAR team in the Arden Arcade neighborhood published a youth-led book of poetry about child abuse and neglect. The young poets used personal stories to direct the community's attention to the issue. Many YPAR teams also doubled as CIL youth leadership teams, building direct block-by-block access and connections to youth voices, leadership, and civic engagement. BCLC teams found an authentic "sweet spot" in listening to youth and building skills to develop health equity solutions that came directly from those most affected by death-bound issues.

BCLC leaders successfully applied to the California Board of State and Community Corrections for several grants to reduce youth gun violence. The spin-off initiative is fondly referred to as "Healing the Hood": its goal to provide comprehensive community violence intervention, prevention, and empowerment strategies for youths, families, and community members living in Sacramento neighborhoods with high levels of intergenerational violence. Healing the Hood now serves as the leading initiative to curb youth gun violence and the crisis response mentality in Sacramento. And that is why, for in 2018 and 2019, there was not a single juvenile gun homicide in the city of Sacramento.

REFERENCE

JanMohamed, Abdul. R., 2005. *The Death-Bound-Subject: Richard Wright's Archaeology of Death*. Durham, NC: Duke University Press.

COMMUNITY-BASED LEADERSHIP

License to Operate at the Intersection
of Love and Humility

Ijeoma Ononuju

I don't remember the time or where I was when I received the phone call that Honesty had been murdered; I just remember the feeling of FEAR. I had been on the job for a couple of months at that point, and I had somehow convinced myself that I might be able to avoid having to deal with any homicides. Honesty's murder became the first of thirteen homicides that would happen over a four-month period in the Heights, and at the time of his death, I was not ready to deal with all that comes with being involved in crisis response. Quite frankly, I was scared, but because he was my first, that brutal initiation would set the course for what my time would be like working in the community for the next two years.

I was hired by the Roberts Family Development Center (RFDC) to be the program director for the Black Child Legacy Campaign's Del Paso Heights/North Sacramento Community Incubator Lead. Unlike the previous program director who had a history of working in the community with RFDC, and who even had run for a school board position, most of my work had been behind-the-scenes and incognito. Thus, I was walking into the work and world of BCLC as a relative unknown to the community and its people. "Dr. O? Who is this Dr. O?" That was the look and feeling that I would get from folks when I started. I could tell that most folks took my name, Dr. O, as a sign of pretentiousness, that I thought I was better than them. Here we go again! Another educated Black person coming into their community with the idea of fixing them. Of condemning them. Of telling them all the things that were wrong, only to eventually leave and forget about them. One day, someone I looked up to as a mentor pulled me aside.

"Ijeoma, why you going around here introducing yourself as Dr. O? You know folks around here don't like that. You not starting off on the right foot. You making a bad name for yourself."

Thank God for her and the few folks who did know me. I borrowed some of their social capital, asking for them to vouch for me until I was able to earn my own. But figuring out how to do that proved difficult. One thing was certain: my postsecondary education credentials were not what would move the community. However, this only deepened my dilemma. How would I earn the kind of trust that would allow me to assume a leadership role within the community? I found the answer the evening of Honesty's death.

If you want to know who you are and where you stand with people, find them in their deepest moment of pain. At least that is what I believe. Because it is in that moment when they don't have time for the shenanigans. No time to be polite to people who haven't earned it. No time to be accommodating to people who are in the way. Just brutal honesty and efficiency in the face of tragedy. For they carry the responsibility for consoling. For healing. For seeking answers to questions that often have no answers. And as I stood out there that summer evening, behind police tape designed to create distance between us and the place where Honesty's body still lay, surrounded by people I didn't know and who didn't care to know me in that moment, I never felt so invisible. Not alone, just invisible.

I had my phone in hand, calling and texting the individuals who made up our Crisis Response Team. The mothers who were all too familiar with how to respond to this type of crisis, one that had ravaged their community for decades. The street soldiers, whose ears were to the ground gathering information as they dealt with their own grief, because they knew the deceased. Even my superiors, who required up-to-date information about the situation. What happened? Who was involved? Do you need anything? Have you contacted the family? Overwhelmed by emotions that I didn't know how to carry and a job for which I was emotionally unprepared, I just wanted to scream HELP ME!!!!! I didn't, but I remember those words ringing in my head. How do you ask for help when you are the help? So, I stood there, standing invisible under a tree, observing the pain and grief of a community, relying on people whom I had only met a few months before to keep me informed about something that many considered to be "family business" and were not keen on outsiders butting in.

When I finally saw someone I recognized, it was a brother I had just met about a week before at the Neighborhood Wellness Center. He was one of the leaders of the mentoring organization, Brother 2 Brother, and was on his way to speak to the police. When I saw him, he said, "What up O, you wanna come with me?" He invited me inside the caution tape, where we met a few of the mothers of the community, one of whom had been all too clear at our first meeting that she didn't like my supervisor and was keeping her eye on me. To my surprise, when I saw her, she greeted me with an endearing "Dr. O," gave me a hug, and said, "We are glad to see you here." In her voice, as well as her hug, was not just grief. I could feel her exhaustion. Physical exhaustion? Yes. Mental, emotional exhaustion? Of course. But this exhaustion was heavier. Looking into her eyes, as she was preoccupied with thoughts about managing the situation, supporting the family, and a million other things that a newcomer like me hadn't even thought of, I saw an exhaustion that came from the accumulation of losses and body blows she has had to endure over a lifetime in this community.

From the level of conversation between her group and the police officers, I gathered as much information as I could before acknowledging to myself that I was in too deep. They were operating on a knowledge base that had taken generations to build. They didn't just know Honesty; they knew all the young men involved. They knew their families, had grown up and went to school with their moms, dads, uncles, aunts. Had spent time in their homes and hanging out in the community. They knew the streets, the cuts, and hiding places. And they had the capital to be able to move in and out of those spaces to operate with a level of precision that I was making messy. Yes, they were willing to bring me along, but I didn't have what they had to be brought along. What they had, you didn't get in a PhD program. You only got that when you devoted your life to a place and a people. So, I whispered to the brotha that I had some candles and water, found out where I could drop them off, and quietly made my exit.

My Journey Begins

The Black Child Legacy Campaign created an unapologetically Black movement in the city of Sacramento with one purpose: *save the lives of Black children.* The power of the initiative was in its embrace of the spirit that "it takes the hood to save the hood" (Watson 2012). Facilitated but not owned by the Sierra Health Foundation, BCLC was instead given to the community, to regular everyday people who were empowered politically, socially, and economically to become the change they sought. It proved to be supremely successful. By the summer of 2019, BCLC had exceeded its target goals for child death reduction in all the focal categories except one, and it was making significant progress in that area too. As a result, some of those who started this movement began to transition into new roles; still others began to transition out altogether. This is where my journey to lead the BCLC Del Paso Heights/North Sacramento Community Incubator Lead (CIL) begins.

As educators, scholars, and educational leaders, we often focus our view of leadership on the individual. As a result, leadership is seen as interchangeable, and institutions are seen as culturally distinct entities from the communities within which they operate. Applying autoethnography (Chang 2016; Hughes and Pennington 2017), I illustrate how my initiation into crisis response, along with my personal educational philosophy, governed how I would interact with the community as I developed in my leadership role. Applying Lave and Wegner's (1991, 1998) framework of legitimate peripheral participation, I use the events surrounding Honesty's death to discuss the challenges of being an outsider working in leadership within an historically established community of practice.

The Heights

The Del Paso Heights (the Heights) community is one of the last Black bastions of Sacramento, with generation upon generation having called the community home. Talk to anyone from the Heights, and not only do they know everyone else who is from the community but they can also tell you their whole genealogy and *the stories* that consist of street names, houses on blocks, who lived with whom, whom they lived with, people who lived on those streets, and all the other personal information that told you about their history and deep community. What stands out about these stories is the proximity between where they were told, the places where they happened, and where those involved still lived. You were always just down the street, around the corner, or on the other side of that block. This is the beauty of this neighborhood.

Place is a multidimensional concept that incorporates the biophysical environment, personal/psychological elements, social and cultural context, and the political/economic milieu (Ardoin 2006). Individually, people experience place through history, culture, geography, and politics. We make sense of our experiences and, by extension, our community based on how we are positioned among the elements of the place (Barton and Berchini 2013). Historically relevant cultural communities may or may not be congruent with political and geographical boundaries, however; because of the conditions in which they were formed, these communities have histories that are imbued with racial identification, oppression, and pride (McAuley 1998). This abstract understanding of place is realized in the Heights. The Heights is as much about the geography as it is about the people. In that sense, its geography adds a dimension to their stories. It is as real and as tangible as the people, the conflict, the struggles, and the victories; in other words, place as identity.

Although rich in history, the Heights is plagued by poverty. Driving around the community, you see its consequences in the pervasiveness of homeless encampments, substance abuse, and dilapidated buildings. Inexpensive when built, housing is now falling victim to the rising costs of living, forcing families to relocate or consolidate because economic insecurity and food insecurity continue to remain problems for so many.

If you are from the Heights, you *love* the Heights. The emotional bond between the people and their environment is real. Despite its challenges, it is the place where they feel comfortable and safe (Hildago and Hernandez 2001). But in that safety exists conflict. Strife that arises from an early age often follows individuals into adulthood. Wounds that occurred decades ago often are never addressed and heal but settle into vitriol that prevents connections, even when goals are shared. The result is you have a community moving in the same direction—but as five fingers as opposed to one fist. Yet even in this division there exists protocol. For outsiders seeking to penetrate the community with the aim of doing work, permission must be granted. Despite the division and disagreement inside the work, all are unified under the banner of their love for that place and their community, and they are extremely protective of them.

Community of Practice and Legitimate Peripheral Participation

As part of my foray into the BCLC universe, I instantly became a participant in three distinct communities of practice (CP), the BCLC CP, which was inclusive of the seven CILs and the Sierra Health Foundation; the Roberts Family Development Center (RFDC) CP; and the Del Paso/North Sacramento CP. Communities of practice "are groups of people who share a concern, set of problems or a passion about a topic, and who deepen their knowledge and expertise in this area by interacting on an ongoing basis" (Lave and Wenger 2001, 124). I focus on my participation in the third of these CPs, because the Heights defies the perception that communities as defined by neighborhood affiliation are not legitimate CPs.

More than anything else, the Heights functions as a CP because it was built around regular interactions between members of the community who deal with the consequences of learning how to survive and build a better community.

Furthermore, these interactions have taken place over decades. The Heights therefore fits into Etienne Wenger (1998)'s identification of the three defining characteristics of a CP: joint enterprise/domain, mutual engagement/community, and shared repertoire/practice.

1. *Joint enterprise/domain* is the shared interest of a group. It "defines the identity of the community, its place in the world and its value to members and others" (Wenger 1998, 195). For the community, this is their negotiated response to their situation, to the conditions in which they are bound; it goes beyond working together to achieve a stated goal, but creates among members a mutual accountability, shared competence, and commitment to the domain that distinguishes members from non-members (see also Floding and Swier 2012).

2. *Mutual engagement/community* is rooted in the idea that culture does not exist in the abstract but is a result of people engaging in joint activities with each other. Culture exists in a community of people and the relations of mutual engagement. Those who engage "help each other, share information, learn together, and build relationships— resulting in a sense of belonging and mutual commitment" (Floding and Swier 2012, 195). As such, members of a CP are committed to figuring out better ways of improving the community for everyone's benefit.

3. *Shared repertoire/practice.* The repertoire of a CP is the culture and all the routines, words, tools, ways of doing things, ways of knowing, stories, gestures, symbols, genres, actions, and concepts of that culture that the community has produced or adopted in the course of its existence. The repetition of these things is what ingrains them within the practice of the community (Floding and Swier 2012).

This is what makes the Heights a unique CP: it is a domain of living and surviving amid challenging social and economic conditions where residents help each other realize a better tomorrow, based on shared practices that define the ways they go about this work. This is also what makes BCLC uniquely successful. Rather than taking a one-size-fits-all approach, it gives ownership of the seven CILs to the communities, allowing them to customize their approach to reducing the deaths of Black children based on their communities of practice. This is also what makes it challenging for an outsider to engage in the work. When a CP has been developed over generations, newcomers cannot just jump in and start leading. More than knowing the domain or the shared repertoire, they must establish their commitment to making the whole better through the community's negotiated set of practices, not their own.

Legitimate peripheral participation orients any entry into a community of practice as a learning experience (Lave and Wegner 1998), precisely the opposite of dominant White notions of leadership. The dominant model is centered around the individual, is hierarchically based and unidirectional, powerfully distinguishes the leader from others, and suggests innate qualities unique to the individual (Simkins 2005). By focusing on the individual, this brand of leadership is seen as transferable, regardless of community or place. Leaders are seen as effective because they emphasize task and not people and relationships (Lomotey 1993; Tillman 2009), and they often approach entry into a CP as one in which they are the primary actor and the CP is a supporting character.

In contrast, entry into a CP from the periphery, as the function of a learning experience, results in the newcomer's legitimacy, regardless of their status, being conferred not by their credentials but by the OGs, elders, and other participants of that community. This can happen in a variety of ways, but what is most important is that the OGs control access to the kinds and levels of participation that the newcomer is permitted to experience (Floding and Swier 2012; Wegner 1998). A key advantage of the legitimate peripheral participation model is that the incoming leader's entrance is facilitated by a willingness to assume the role of learner, giving the OGs an opportunity to own the role of expert and begin to teach and help the new leader discern what is essential and important (Floding and Swier 2012).

A second advantage is that, as new leaders enter the community, they do so with a new perspective, one that is generally welcomed by the OGs. However, this gift must be given in accordance with the legitimacy and access conferred to them by the OGs. In other words, the new leaders must understand that the sharing of their perspective must be moderated by their level of participation and acceptance in the community. As they are drawn further into the community and are given permission to practice their craft, their level of mastery and competence in the practices of the community grows deeper along with their level of authenticity and belonging.

Educational Leadership Philosophy

My leadership philosophy stems from my identity as a scholar and educator. Borrowing from the literature on Black school principals, my educational leadership philosophy is based on what Kofi Lomotey (1993) calls the "ethno-humanist" role. Leaders who operate within this role are defined by their commitment to the community they serve, carry confidence in the ability of those they serve to achieve, and embody a compassion for and understanding of the structural in-

COMMUNITY-BASED LEADERSHIP   99

equities that frame communities. Mark Gooden (2005, 649) notes that these leaders lean on their ethno-humanist role to remain "engaged as he or she struggle[d] to transform a situation of despair and hopelessness into one of infinite possibilities." Leaders who occupy this form of leadership focus on service through interpersonal care where the primary goals are met through acknowledgment of a set of cultural goals (Tillman 2009).

One reason why I use the legitimate peripheral participation framework is that, as a scholar and educator, learning is at the core of my work. But there is more than learning involved: healing serves as the foundation on which I focus the outcomes of my work. Education and learning are the mediums through which I am healed and I heal, with healing being the intentional process of humanity restoration. In other words, my work is about trying to restore what has been stolen: our humanity. This is the quintessential work of BCLC. When a mother comes into our office, vulnerable because she is housing insecure, food insecure, or job insecure, she is saying to us that she needs to be restored. Her healing becomes our priority in all the areas of her life that we can affect.

This is the job. Leadership is to be expressed not through actions that highlight self but through selfless service that seeks to acknowledge our full humanity. Fundamentally, this requires humility and love. *Humility* because as I assume the role of learner, I am freely admitting the areas in which I am not whole. My work is not a function of knowing the answers but of knowing how to seek the answers. Thus, the job becomes a cycle of lessons and self-assessments, where each day my service is dependent on my ability as a leader to learn from those I serve so that I may serve even more effectively. And *love* because, as Martin Luther King Jr., reminds us, "power at its best is love implementing the demands of justice." Without love, there is no justice, just reckless and abusive power, the actualization of which becomes oppression. That is why I follow the ethno-humanist expression of leadership: at the core of this work is the demand to fight for a justice that will transform the lives of those I serve.

"Legitimate" Is Preceded by an Invitation

> When I saw him, he said "What up O, you wanna come with me?" He invited me inside the caution tape, where we met a few of the mothers of the community . . .

At the time of Honesty's death, although I knew I had to lead our area's Crisis Response Team, I still did not understand what that role should look like. When I came on the scene, my feelings of invisibility were generated by the questions

I was posing to myself: Did I belong here? If so, where? How exactly did I belong? Legitimacy of participation takes on a form that defines ways of belonging "and is therefore not only a crucial condition for learning, but a constitutive element of its content" (Lave and Wegner 1998, 35).

One mistake that a new leader cannot afford to make when entering a new CP is to fail to recognize the power relations and social structures that existed before he or she came along. It is not merely the legitimacy of participation that is at stake but also the legitimacy of peripherality. In all communities of practice, there exist formal and informal social structures and power relations that carry the history of the community whose members, as a consequence of their lived experiences with both pain and victory, possess the right to grant permission of entry and participation and to validate the new leader's position, access, and level of participation.

On the evening of Honesty's death, I was given permission in the form of the invitation from one of the elders behind the caution tape. With that simple invitation, my presence at the crisis was given legitimacy, and I received the answers to my questions of whether and how I belonged. The concept of belonging is a powerful and important value to leadership because it speaks to identity and the ability of a leader to identify with those he or she serves.[1]

"Peripheral" Sometimes Equates to Invisibility and Exits

Yes, they were willing to bring me along, but I didn't have what they had to be brought along.

Legitimate peripherality and peripheral participation are about understanding your place and position within the community, and the two work in tandem with each other. For me, this is where the concept of servitude comes into play. On the one hand, legitimate peripherality is the validation I received to be on the periphery to do the work; its legitimacy derives from the power structure or eldership of the community. On that evening, only the elder's invitation behind the tape carried weight because he represented someone who had access and authority.

My peripheral participation is about knowing the role I was given permission to participate in and understanding that permission from one or a few did not equate to consensus throughout the community. I took my leadership as an expression of servitude to mean that serving did not require me to be heard or seen, that there are moments when I must decrease so that the community can increase. For me on that night, service was not about taking credit, being seen, or being in the mix; it was about remaining invisible and giving space to those who were grieving. My instincts told me that, as a function of my newcomer status, this is what was most important: that my leadership was about maximizing my contribution while minimizing the potential of becoming a distraction. It was important that I took this stance because, even though I had received permission to be there, my work had yet to be validated. Although some of the elders knew who I was, I was still an unknown for most of the community. Furthermore, I knew that only my work could validate my presence as our conversations would become more intimate and sensitive. My credentials had no value; they did not earn me a license to operate.

"Participation" Is Facilitated by the Service of Care, Compassion, and Commitment

> To my surprise, when I saw her, she greeted me with an endearing "Dr. O," gave me a hug and said, "We are glad to see you here." In her voice, as well as her hug, was not just grief. You could feel her exhaustion.

Although I presented legitimate participation and peripheral participation as separate ideas, they really act in concert with one another. There can be no legitimate participation without peripheral participation. The legitimacy of my participation on the night of Honesty's death was facilitated by a recognition that, by my peripheral participation, I understood my place and position. One cannot occur without the other, but there is no set order in which they must take place. This is often the mistake that new leaders make when they enter a community of practice: either they expect permission without offering peripheral participation, or their work and participation are not appropriately peripheral, in that they begin operating within boundaries for which they have not been given permission and thus their participation is not legitimate.

Legitimate peripheral participation is less about what you do and more about how. The way I showed up that night and in the days and weeks that followed is what resonated most with the community. It was not what I did but how I showed up. When I first arrived in the Heights in my new role, community members frankly told me that they had been observing me. As an outsider, they paid attention to the work I was doing, how I approached the work, and how I held myself when interacting with the community. So, when the community mother greeted me that evening, the endearing nature of her greeting, followed by a hug, was recognition that I had shown up correctly. The how of my crisis response revolved around three distinct components: showing up, showing compassion, and serving with care.

Showing up is the first step because it demonstrates commitment to the community and the work. In that moment, I was afraid that I was not mentally prepared to deal with the emotions caused by a homicide, and I was worried about the spiritual toll that the violence of that event would take on me. Walking within the inner sanctum of a still-foreign community, when everyone is on edge and there are active concerns of continued violence and retaliation, was challenging, but approaching the situation and my peripherality within it with humility made it possible to show up in a way the community needed. The other elements that informed my participation—compassion and care—then allowed me to serve a grieving community. The community mother's embrace of me embodied her grief and exhaustion. My role, guided by compassion and care, was to be open to her vulnerability and her pain.

Implications

As an educational leader, it is critical to understand how leaders show up in new communities. My new role with BCLC therefore was an opportunity not only to serve the Heights community but also to test out the framework and ideas I had been theorizing as a scholar and now had to put into place as a leader. Did my approach have any positive impact on the community's ability to heal or on our primary objective of reducing juvenile homicides in Sacramento? I believe our work has enabled the community to heal from legacies of violence, but its impact is less conclusive in regard to homicide reduction.

One of the tragedies of the two-plus years of the COVID-19 pandemic is that we simultaneously experienced a gun violence epidemic in the United States and in Sacramento. During the summer of 2020, Sacramento experienced twice the number of homicides than the previous year. It was not a coincidence that during one of the most difficult times in our recent history—as people were losing jobs, as families were struggling, as we isolated from each other, and as we watched images of violence against Black bodies stream across our phones, computers, and TVs—anger erupted in our communities. Hurt people hurt people—usually those in closest proximity. For those in the BCLC in that moment, our work was never harder, and the resources were never more meager. As a result, it is difficult to quantify the impact that my approach had on our ability to prevent any more Honestys from losing their lives. But my framework did earn me the respect of the community, which in turn enabled me to respond and do the work required in that moment.

This story is not my story. It belongs to Honesty, who lost his life far too young. It belongs to his mother, whom we worked with and assisted in the weeks afterward, trying to ensure that her humanity was restored. It also belongs to the other young men and women who lost their lives to violence and poverty and the systemic inequity that plague our community. And in many ways, it belongs to the community warriors—the mothers, the fathers, the ministers, the advocates, the youth, and the folks who do not get to tap out and escape. This story and hundreds of others like it are the essence of why BCLC exists.

NOTE

1. For Lomotey (1989), cultural affiliations and a leader's ability to identify with those they serve have a direct correlation with the care they give.

REFERENCES

Ardoin, Nicole M. 2006. "Toward an Interdisciplinary Understanding of Place: Lessons for Environmental Education." *Canadian Journal of Environmental Education* 11, no. 1: 112–126.

Barton, Angela Carabrese, and Christina Berchini. 2013. "Becoming an Insider: Teaching Science in Urban Settings." *Theory into Practice* 52, no. 1: 21–27.

Chang, Heewon. 2016. *Autoethnography as Method*, vol. 1. New York: Routledge.

Floding, Matthew, and Glen Swier. 2011. "Legitimate Peripheral Participation: Entering a Community of Practice." *Reflective Practice: Formation and Supervision in Ministry* 31: 193–204.

Gooden, Mark A. 2005. "The Role of an African American Principal in an Urban Information Technology High School." *Educational Administration Quarterly* 41, no. 4: 630–650.

Hidalgo, M. Carmen, and Bernardo Hernandez. 2001. "Place Attachment: Conceptual and Empirical Questions." *Journal of Environmental Psychology* 21, no. 3: 273–281.

Hughes, Sherick A., and Julie Pennington. 2016. *Autoethnography: Process, Product, and Possibility for Critical Social Research*. Thousand Oaks: SAGE.

Lave, Jean, and Etienne Wenger. 1991. *Situated Learning: Legitimate Peripheral Participation*. Cambridge: Cambridge University Press.

Lave, Jean, and Etienne Wenger. 1998. "Legitimate Peripheral Participation." In *Learners, Learning, and Assessment*, edited by Patricia Murphy, 111–126. Thousand Oaks, CA: SAGE.

Lave, Jean, and Etienne Wenger. 2001. "Legitimate Peripheral Participation in Communities of Practice." In *Supporting Lifelong Learning*, edited by Julia Clarke, Ann Hanson, Roger Harrison, and Fiona Reeve. London: Routledge.

Lomotey, Kofi. 1989. *African-American Principals: School Leadership and Success*. Westport, CT: Greenwood Press.

Lomotey, Kofi. 1993. "African-American Principals: Bureaucrat/Administrators and Ethno-humanists." *Urban Education* 27, no. 4: 394–412.

McAuley, William J. 1998. "History, Race, and Attachment to Place among Elders in the Rural All-Black Towns of Oklahoma." *Journals of Gerontology Series B: Psychological Sciences and Social Sciences* 53: no. 1: 535–545.

Simkins, Tim. 2005. "Leadership in Education: 'What Works' or 'What Makes Sense'?" *Educational Management Administration and Leadership* 33, no. 1: 9–26.

Tillman, Linda C. 2009. "African American Principals and the Legacy of Brown." In *The SAGE Handbook of African American Education*, edited by Linda C. Tillman, 171–204. Thousand Oaks, CA: SAGE.

Watson, Vajra. 2012. *Learning to Liberate: Community-Based Solutions to the Crisis in Urban Education*. London: Taylor & Francis.

Wenger, Etienne. 1999. *Communities of Practice: Learning, Meaning, and Identity*. Cambridge: Cambridge University Press.

THE PAST MEETS THE PRESENT

Inside The Build.Black. Coalition

Kindra F. Montgomery-Block

I am not worried when things are bubbling uncomfortably in a community; unrest means that there is power up for grabs, and we have to be ready to grab it!
—Chet P. Hewitt, CEO of the Sierra Health Foundation

The Black Child Legacy Campaign (BCLC) is an initiative of the Center of Health Program Management of the Sierra Health Foundation. Build. Black., an extension of BCLC, focuses on ecnomic mobility and stability within the African American community (see the appendix for its vison and pillars). Its goal is to build economic opportunities in Sacramento County for Black communities through a focus on health, entrepreneurship, youth voice, and jobs. It is one umbrella that unifies us. Build.Black. is also the professional and personal working together. Build.Black. is a community-led solution to address our pain, fortify our power, celebrate our history, and build legacy. Build.Black. is when the past meets the present.

Build.Black. is rooted in the tragic police killing of Stephon Clark in March 2018 in his grandmother's backyard in Meadowview, a South Sacramento neighborhood. Sacramento police and sheriffs had mistakenly identified Stephon as a threat and a property vandal. The officers shot Clark, firing 20 rounds, believing that had pointed a gun at them. Police found only a cell phone on him. This unjust killing by local law enforcement ignited a flame of unrest in the city of Sacramento. His death began a slew of protestation and riots that forced the closing of Sacramento's Golden 1 Center Arena, where the NBA Kings play their home games. His death also marked a hard pivot in our city, awakening justice activists and creating a civil rights movement.

Build.Black. begin with an urgent Sunday morning call to Chet Hewitt, CEO of the Sierra Health Foundation. It was a warm day in March on the weekend after the police killed Clark. The BCLC "community pulse" barometer was way up on the end of "something horrific is about to happen." Chet had his ear close to the "community folks," and in our early morning check-in, we agreed that we needed to do something quickly to provide a sense of leadership in the face of the upcoming storm. Indeed, Sacramento and Stephon Clark's unjust killing made national and international news overnight. Many so-called civil rights leaders showed up the next day unannounced to provide media interviews, align themselves with the Clark family, and speak on behalf of Black Sacramento and "our" collective needs; their actions only served to create deep rifts among local leaders. It was clear that we had to organize ourselves and present our demands to improve our city. The BCLC, although it was authentically connected to racial justice change, needed help.

Chet called his mentor, the health equity and racial justice guru Angela Glover Blackwell, founder and CEO of Policy Link. This was an "emergency community call"—different from a 911 call but on the same lifesaving level. Glover Blackwell is world renowned for her leadership on policies and strategies that transform vulnerable communities. She advised our team on how to move forward to engage community partners and immediately deescalate some of the unrest created by overpolicing. She agreed to host a community listening session at the Sierra Health Foundation early the same week. But what stunned the BCLC team was the first question she asked: "What are the current infighting issues among leaders in the African American community?" We were stunned—and impressed. How did she know about the infighting in the community? Because she is a national elder and she had dealt with many issues of police injustice and community unrest. Her goal was to coach us to make sure that we first dealt with the social and emotional needs of our people and partners. We were calling her for guidance out of a sense of desperation—and she knew the first play.

That Sunday evening, we hosted a meeting in the Sierra Health Foundation board room, providing Chinese food for twelve trusted Black civil rights leaders, those familiar in the community for their efforts and sustained advocacy, positioned to address racial and ethnic equity and inclusive collective action in pursuit of justice for Stephon Clark and Black Sacramento. They included local leaders from the NAACP, Urban League, Black Lives Matter, California Urban Partnership, Sistalect, Roberts Family Development Center, South Sacramento Christian Center, Voice of the Youth, and Activism Articulated. Build.Black. was born out of that meeting and the commitments made by those leaders. In that Sunday evening meeting, they were able to establish the tenets and vision that have unified our community and charted a path for economic prosperity. The next day, the Build.Black. leadership stood shoulder to shoulder at press conferences and City Council meetings to present the program's goals to unite our community and its political demands, wearing BCLC t-shirts and buttons and carrying signs that boldly declared the call for a renewed focus on economic justice.

Build.Black. stands today as Sacramento's foremost inclusive community economic development collaboration. In Chet Hewitt's words, "You can do all the good health and racial justice impact programs you want. The influence that BCLC has will only be surface deep. It still won't be enough for impoverished Black communities to really change, because we have to show people how to get out of the cycle of poverty." And this is exactly what Build.Black was created to do: to complement the social safety-net infrastructure of the BCLC and drive inclusive economic development in targeted vulnerable neighborhoods.

The Build.Black. Coalition is a successful example of change philanthropy and moving the community to action, made possible by the BCLC's leadership role in the community, the infrastructure it created, and its deep relationships with stakeholders and community leaders. Through our collective efforts we have secured funding and created a Black entrepreneur partnership with the City of Sacramento. Over the past four years we have built new and ongoing programs with the Sacramento Kings focused on Black youth in sports and leadership. We have held forums and summits to listen and build community voice. We have shaped local policy and aligned our values to respond to the COVID-19 quarantine and helped businesses cope with it. We have also purchased property and hope to expand our micro-enterprise initiatives.

Build.Black. has connected Black neighborhoods and service providers across Sacramento County. The limited resources that many Black-led community–based organizations (CBOs) face when working in isolation no longer prevents full-family, wraparound service support. Through the strategic design and infrastructure of the BCLC, the social service safety net has been restructured to serve vulnerable Black families and create economic prosperity.

Yet, in the summer of 2022, Chet Hewitt felt moved to write to Sacramento's municipal leadership demanding renewed funding for many of Build.Black.'s initiatives, including its Youth Pop-Up program, designed to expand on the success of the Healing the Hood program in reducing youth violence, providing an effective crisis response, and offering diverse youth services. Only four years after the death of Stephon Clark, everything that the Black community had been fighting for seemed to be suddenly on the budgetary chopping block. Racial justice and health equity victories seemed to be forgotten, encouraging data about program successes were being questioned or doubted, and rivalry politics were overshadowing community needs.

This backsliding often happened before, but social justice work can be overwhelmingly burdensome because of the need to keep "fighting the good fight" with such predictable and frustrating setbacks. Yet, the models provided by Chet Hewitt and the Build.Black. Coalition will continue to give hope and power to the people.

Appendix
Build.Black. Coalition: Vision and Pillars, March 2018

Vision Statement

- To transform our neighborhoods through strategic economic development for the residents most impacted.
- It takes the community to save the community. Those closes pain are best to drive solutions.
- We are implementing a community economic vision that is specific to the needs and attributes of Black communities.
- Build bridges to the people and businesses to Sacramento's economic renaissance.

Pillars to Unite Our Communities

- Uplifting Black youth voices
- Health equity and access
- Justice and policing in Black communities
- Investment in Black neighborhoods and businesses

Part 4
LIFE

How do we move from theory to practice? How do we connect our head, heart, and feet? These questions cannot be answered through a training or toolkit, but in how we actually move in this world. For this reason, "Part 4. Life" centers on the real lives of real people remembering, reckoning, and reimagining racial justice with each breath and every step. Through their portraits we can show, not just tell, the intimate and intricate nature of movement building. The personal is political, and for Phil, Chet, Kindra, Crystal, and Jackie their incredible on-the-ground work in Sacramento is more than a job: it is their intergenerational purpose, lifeline, and legacy.

METHODOLOGY MATTERS
The Power of Portraiture

Vajra M. Watson

Research is not a stand-alone mirror of reality but a kaleidoscope comprising tiny fragments of mirrors and shards of colored glass that, when pointed toward the light, reflect off one another, forming magical patterns. Who holds the kaleidoscope is meaningful because what gets included is as important as what gets omitted. With the slightest turn of the wrist, the final image can completely change. Regardless of methodology, researchers make significant decisions that inform the data that take shape to then inform the findings. As a process of scientific inquiry, our research used each person's frame of reference, including our own, to shape—but not solely reflect—the final pictures that formed the portraits in chapters 13–17.

Because research is personal, purposeful, and political, the methods we use to investigate our questions are as important as the findings. To humanize the data collection process, we relied on *portraiture*—a qualitative research methodology that bridges science and art—to merge "the systematic and careful description of good ethnography with the evocative resonance of fine literature" (Lawrence-Lightfoot 2005, 6). Portraiture is rooted in a style of vivid storytelling that allows the reader into the moment. This kind of account permits a multifaceted reality to unfold that feels, and is, alive and authentic.

Developed by Sara Lawrence-Lightfoot, portraiture seeks to unveil the universal truths and resonant stories that lie in the specifics and complexity of everyday life. *The Art and Science of Portraiture* by Sara Lawrence-Lightfoot and Jessica Hoffmann Davis (1997) is a seminal text of this relatively new methodology that illuminates the complex dynamics and subtlety of human experience and organizational life. The work of Lawrence-Lightfoot, the visionary who developed this qualitative research process, becomes a roadmap for ideas and insights about how to develop the arc of an investigation. Her scholarship serves as a source of inspiration for the growing number of social scientists who use her methods (e.g., Chapman 2007; Harding 2005; Hill 2005; Ononuju 2016).

To humanize the people within the Black Child Legacy Campaign, their portraits were carefully crafted. The depth of writing was meant to show, rather than tell, the process of transformation and empowerment unveiled by the data. According to Lawrence-Lightfoot, portraiture is a practice of emancipation, unfolding in the form of human archaeology. As a qualitative tool, our methods share commonalities with ethnography and narrative inquiry, but differ in five distinct ways:

1. Portraitists are not simply "flies on the wall," we are ever-present and lend our voice to the narrative that unfolds.
2. Portraitists use the entirety of their being to unearth answers to complex questions told through the lives of individuals who embody some semblance of the answers.
3. Portraitists explicitly guard against fatalistic, pessimistic inquiries into problems, instead searching for solutions by examining nuances of goodness.
4. Portraitists do not make participants anonymous, nameless factors but seek to acknowledge, honor, and validate their stories by using the real names of people and places.
5. Portraitists are committed to sharing findings that are accessible to audiences beyond the academy as an explicit act of community building.

Guided by these pillars, portraiture allows a soulful narrative to emerge—yet this does not imply subjectivism. Drawing mainly from grounded theory, we used various tools to systematically analyze the data. First, to ensure descriptive validity, we tape recorded and transcribed all interviews verbatim, including words like "um . . ." and "you know." We processed field notes within one day of observation and conducted an initial open coding. Second, we wrote reflexive memos and kept journals. We approached the interview data aware that they were representative of a process of co-construction in which teller and listener create meaning collaboratively. Through writing memos and journal entries, we kept strict notes of our personal impressions and thoughts as we gathered information. Third, to ensure interpretive validity, we systematically emphasized evidence in analytic memos and narrative summaries by citing participants' own words and documenting transcript page numbers to connect our interpretations to the data. We compared discrepant data to working observations to assess whether to consider alternative explanations. Fourth, we conducted member checks by having participants review their interview transcripts and clarify or expand on any issue raised. These strategies are important tools for developing validity and for guarding against researcher bias. Fifth, we triangulated across several data sources—participant observation, questionnaires, interviews, surveys, and supplemental documentation—to reduce the risk of chance associations and biases due to data collection methods. Sixth, we solicited feedback regularly from colleagues who were skilled researchers but were not intimately connected to the data. We shared transcripts, memos, and matrices with them to identify discrepant data and to strengthen our coding strategies and analytic tools. Such alternative interpretations are necessary to forge accurate findings and proper conclusions. Seventh, we mined the data for seeds of the solution that could be replicated and sustained. This final process ensures that the answers to our questions inform a greater good. For those that are interested, suggested readings on portraiture as a research methodology can be found after the References.

As we pivot to the portraits, please consider the metaphor of a tree. Much research focuses on the leaves: the facts and figures that are byproducts of certain kinds of work. Then there are studies that emphasize the branches—those correlations of how, why, and where the leaves connect. And there are plenty of studies that simultaneously consider the historical context: the roots. Our focus in this part, however, was on digging (literally and figuratively) through years of information and layers of discoveries, constantly triangulating among multiple sources, to uncover the seed of the story—for it is the seed that holds the soul of the work, its essence. Building on this idea of a tree, neither policy makers nor practitioners can plant a tree only with leaves, limbs, or roots. To grow this work in Sacramento and beyond, seeds need to be planted, nourished, and cultivated. It is the people who plant these seeds.

To honor these individuals, we made every attempt to depict their effectiveness in a way that is nuanced, accurate, and authentic. If we failed to accomplish this, we take full responsibility; these movement makers within the Black Child Legacy Campaign became vulnerable to us so that they might become real to you. Let's turn to them now.

REFERENCES

Chapman, Thandeka K. 2007. "Interrogating Classroom Relationships and Events: Using Portraiture and Critical Race Theory in Education Research." *Educational Researcher* 36, no. 3: 156–162.

Harding, H. A. 2005. "'City Girl': A Portrait of a Successful White Urban Teacher." *Qualitative Inquiry* 11: no. 1: 52–80.

Hill, Djanna A. 2005. "The Poetry in Portraiture: Seeing Subjects, Hearing Voices, and Feeling Contexts." *Qualitative Inquiry* 11, no. 1: 95–105.

Lawrence-Lightfoot, Sara. 2005. "Reflections on Portraiture: A Dialogue between Art and Science." *Qualitative Inquiry* 11, no. 1: 3–15.

Lawrence-Lightfoot, Sara, and Jessica Hoffmann Davis. 1997. *The Art and Science of Portraiture*. San Francisco: Jossey-Bass.

Ononuju, Ijeoma E. 2016. "Black Portraits: The Leadership Practices of Four Secondary Male Administrators." PhD diss., University of California, Davis.

FURTHER READING ON PORTRAITURE

Behar, Ruth. 2014. *The Vulnerable Observer: Anthropology that Breaks Your Heart*. Boston: Beacon Press.

Catone, Keith C. 2017. *The Pedagogy of Teacher Activism: Four Portraits for Justice*. New York: Peter Lang.

Chapman, Thandeka K. 2005. "Expressions of 'Voice' in Portraiture." *Qualitative Inquiry* 11, no. 1: 27–51.

Erickson, Frederick. 2016. "First, Do No Harm: A Comment." *Anthropology and Education Quarterly* 47, no. 1: 100–103.

Glesne, Corrine. 1989. "Rapport and Friendship in Ethnographic Research." *International Journal of Qualitative Studies in Education* 2, no. 1: 45–54.

Lawrence-Lightfoot, Sara. 1983. *The Good High School: Portraits of Character and Culture*. New York: Basic Books.

Lawrence-Lightfoot, Sara. 1988. *Balm in Gilead: Journey of a Healer*. Boston: Addison-Wesley.

Lawrence-Lightfoot, Sara. 1994. *I've Known Rivers: Lives of Loss and Liberation*. Boston: Addison-Wesley.

Lawrence-Lightfoot, Sara. 1999. *Respect: An Exploration*. New York: Perseus Books.

Maxwell, Joseph A. 1996. *Qualitative Research Design: An Interactive Approach*. Thousand Oaks, CA: SAGE.

Paris, Django, and Maisha T. Winn, eds. 2013. *Humanizing Research: Decolonizing Qualitative Inquiry with Youth and Communities*. Thousand Oaks, CA: SAGE.

Smith, Linda T. 1999. *Decolonizing Methodologies: Research and Indigenous peoples*. Dunedin: University of Otago Press.

Watson, Vajra. 2012. *Learning to Liberate: Community-Based Solutions to the Crisis in Urban Education*. New York: Routledge.

Watson, Vajra. 2014. *The Black Sonrise: Oakland Unified School District's Commitment to Address and Eliminate Institutionalized Racism*. Final evaluation report submitted to Oakland Unified School District's Office of African American Male Achievement. http://www.ousd.org/Page/12267.

Watson, Vajra. 2018. *Transformative Schooling: Towards Racial Equity in Education*. New York: Routledge.

Watson, Vajra. 2019. "Liberating Methodologies: Reclaiming Research as a Site for Radical Inquiry and Transformation." In *Community-Based Participatory Research: Testimonios from Chicana/o Studies*, edited by Natalia Deeb-Sossa, 70–88. Tucson: University of Arizona Press.

PEOPLE POWER

Councilmember Phil Serna

Vajra M. Watson

Supervisor Phil Serna's reputation precedes him. Yes, he is in the spotlight as a political figure, but more than that, he is a homegrown leader within the Sacramento community. Phil grew up in the Curtis Park neighborhood and attended local schools. He is the son of Sacramento's first Latino mayor, Joe Serna Jr.

Phil's understanding of public service came from his immediate family and the United Farm Workers, led by Cesar Chavez and Delores Huerta. Early experiences with activism with farmworkers and other organizing groups shaped his career trajectory. He says, "Growing up in a home where civic engagement was a part of everyday life, I learned at a young age that it is not enough to sit on the sidelines and let government happen to you."

In June 2018, voters reelected Serna to a third term as supervisor of the First District on the Sacramento County Board of Supervisors. The 112-square mile district that Phil represents extends from the Sacramento-Sutter County line south to Florin Road, east of Power Inn Road, and from the Sacramento River it stretches east to Watt Avenue. He oversees both the Sacramento International Airport and older established neighborhoods such as South Oak Park. Phil's reach is broad, and he considers it a "privilege to serve" and is proud to representing "one of the region's most diverse constituencies."

As supervisor, Serna has a commendable collaborative work ethic and political track record. A recurring question Phil asks himself is, "How do we improve the quality of life for *all* Sacramento residents?" He recognizes that the answer is not one-dimensional because the underlying problems *and* solutions are systemic.

According to Phil, improving the overall health of Sacramento is not the responsibility of any one person, organization, or institution. His ideas are interdisciplinary and his ambitions cooperative. For any policy to take root and solve real-life problems, it must involve various stakeholders and encompass an intergenerational, multitiered approach—as exemplified by the Black Child Legacy Campaign (BCLC). Phil was instrumental in bringing this movement to life throughout the region, and I am eager to learn more from him. I am particularly interested in the ways he, as a Latino leader, serves as an outspoken and unapologetic champion for Black life. At his office in downtown Sacramento, we delve deep into dialogue. I am curious to learn more about his perspective on racial injustice in Sacramento.

A Place to Exhale

I make my way from my home in Natomas to 700 H Street in Sacramento. Traffic is light, but parking is difficult. I meander through the downtown area until I find a metered parking spot on this brisk fall day in October. I walk as fast as I can to make it to my 10:00 A.M. appointment with Supervisor Serna. As I make my way toward the Sacramento County Administration Center, I am taken aback by its jailhouse demeanor: it is concrete on top of concrete. The institutional milieu of this edifice is heavy, even intimidating. I straighten my blazer, open the large tinted-glass door, and begin looking for Room 2450.

When I reach Supervisor Serna's office, I am relieved by its ambiance and welcoming staff. Although his political work is embedded within this large administration building, Phil's own work area appears in stark contrast. I write in my notebook: *Like an oasis. A place to exhale.*

Phil's office decor is colorful and musically themed; he has guitars near his desk. I am not surprised to learn that he plays the bass and the drums with several local bands. I also know from following him on social media for many years that he enjoys fly fishing and prides himself on cooking elegant and exquisite meals for his wife Roxanna. Underneath this public persona is a thoughtful servant-leader and ambitious agent of change.

In 2011, Phil was considered a "freshman supervisor" because he had only been serving for a few months. Although he was very new to the position, he had no interest in maintaining the status quo. His goal, quite admirably, was to make an impact. Phil's ideals and political acumen were tested when he received a shocking report detailing extreme inequities in Sacramento, the city that raised him.

The study that came to Phil's attention was an analysis of childhood health and well-being in Sacramento from 1990 to 2010. Demonstrating painful patterns and startling statistics, and aptly called the "Child Death Report," it highlighted the fact that African American children were dying at twice the rate of any other children (102 deaths per 100,000 children). Phil had a visceral reaction to this information: "my anger" came from the "fact that Sacramento County" has this "incredible disparity in the number of deaths between African American children and children of other races." This was not about "any given year": there was a pattern of inequality, Phil says. "It has been chronic!" He felt compelled to do something: "I really made the case that this is our number one issue in Sacramento County."

The longitudinal evidence in the report served as a catalyst for honest and courageous conversations. Why do we accept racial disparities as the status quo? Why is preventable death for Black children intergenerational? Even though Supervisor Serna was committed to action, he did not have the answers.

Supervisor Serna also recognized his own limitations: "Child welfare is not my background. I'm an urban planner." He thus decided to get experts into the room and established the Blue Ribbon Commission on Disproportionate African American Child Deaths "comprised of health and child welfare professionals, law enforcement, clergy, mothers, grandmothers, and fathers" to create a "collective focus" and "understand the problem a bit more" as depicted in the "death reports." "Not only understanding the nature of the problem, the challenge, its history," he explains, "but also moving forward. The group continued to ask, 'What do we do about it?'"

The Blue Ribbon Commission built momentum to address the welfare of Black children and youth in Sacramento, yet even this group of experts felt that they lacked the understanding needed to create a full semblance of a strategy. So, they "took it on the road." I ask for clarification. He responds, "We went to various neighborhoods, those neighborhoods [where] the death report tells us the disparity is the greatest" and began to share the data. In listening sessions held in these communities, emotions were stirred, and deeper wounds were revealed. He continues, "I think, anecdotally, everyone kind of understood where the tough neighborhoods are in Sacramento County" and "most deaths associated with violence occur." But something significantly shifted when we had "hard data." In the twenty-first century, racial demographics still greatly shape a child's probability of survival.

Black families in Sacramento County were angry, "which is totally understandable . . . they had never known about this, they had never heard about it!" There was an assumption, among all of us, that "children in Sacramento County basically have access to the same types of health care and parents have access to the same type of education." Supervisor Serna underscores that the "anger people expressed was very palpable." It was also "cathartic for a lot of folks."

He shakes his head and looks down at his desk. He admits, "it was cathartic for me." He utters these words quietly and then asks a rhetorical question: "How do we address the most intimate problems that we have?" The word *intimate* lands between us. The intimacy of race relations in this country, the remnants of all that is still wrong, *here.*

Although political activism and government service were integral to Supervisor Serna's upbringing, for many communities of color—and for Black folks in Sacramento, in particular—politics is not synonymous with productive, collective people power. Too many times, politicians have endorsed, enforced, and rationalized institutional racism. Although it was hard for Supervisor Serna to hear families openly discuss their disdain for city politics, these were truths he needed to hear and to acknowledge. Perhaps a lot of leaders might have stopped there, content with having received feedback from constituents. Supervisor Serna, however, was not satisfied with simply knowing about the problem. He felt responsible for doing something. Momentum continued to build, and he was determined to make a difference.

I try to dig into the details and find out what were his next steps. I ask, "How did you go from facilitating the commission to really creating a line item in the budget and moving the bureaucracy, so to speak, to align with the will of the people?" Phil says emphatically, "I really kind of view myself as *not* doing the heavy lifting, quite frankly. . . . I'll be very honest. It was all the folks around the table—literally, figuratively, with the Blue Ribbon Commission—that really gave a lot of thought to, um . . . [Phil reaches for a metaphor and connects it to a meal] . . . bite off a chunk of meat that we can chew and swallow." That is how the problems of childhood deaths got distilled into "four leading causes of death" and BCLC began to get a foothold with funding. "I'm a big believer that our budgets—your tax dollars—should be reflective of our value sets." At each milestone, Phil understood his position: "For me, politically, it was keeping this issue at the forefront of our discussions, and when I say our discussions, I mean the Board of Supervisors." In addition to his advocacy, Phil remained active as chair of the Blue Ribbon Commission, "quite frankly, kind of [laying] down a challenge to folks to tell me what's a more pressing problem."

There really was no precedent for any of these actions. Yet, these collective efforts were very successful. Early on, individuals were forced to make the road by walking it. Eventually, "gradually, more and more" people joined the walking, the doing of this important work, and Supervisor Serna describes a shift from "talk" to "application." Just *this* step took eighteen months, he admits. "It didn't happen immediately." Shaking his head, he repeats, "That was an eighteen-month process."

To recap, the strategies used to build this city-wide initiative were simple but very effective. Supervisor Serna established a commission that included a wide range of stakeholders. This commission examined the "death report" and shared information via listening sessions with the community. Members of the commission then reached consensus around key focus areas and recommendations. Supervisor Serna recalls, "The ultimate goal, quite frankly, was to reduce African American child deaths 10 to 20% . . . pretty intense accountability that we set for ourselves." At this point, there was created a permanent committee, the Steering Committee on the Reduction of African American Child Deaths, to "dig a little deeper" into the budget and "make specific recommendations for the Board of Supervisors." Supervisor Serna gets serious: "We're talking tens of millions of dollars, and we didn't want this to be an instance where people felt like we're just throwing money at a problem." Finally, a vote among the city supervisors was held, and the funding was approved.

These actions occurred primarily at the policy level, helping catalyze a larger journey toward racial justice in Sacramento. Once the funding was approved, the real work began. Supervisor Serna has long understood that impact must be tangible on the ground, inside people's homes and neighborhoods. Yet, even with good intentions and some institutional support, a gap between city government, social services, and Black families persisted. To gain access and build trust, partner agencies such as the Sierra Health Foundation and Community Incubator Leads became critical conduits for engagement, advocacy, and empowerment.

Bullets Hit Black Children Differently

The work grew exponentially, so I wonder about pushback. Race-based policies that support Black life are still controversial. Supervisor Serna was not distracted by the debates and is still convinced that a specialized approach benefits all of Sacramento. His analysis reminds me of targeted universalism, a framework developed through john a. powell's (2009) extensive legal scholarship on structural racism. Essentially, *targeted universalism* alters the approach of universal strategies—policies that make no distinctions among recipients—to achieve goals such as improved health: it instead argues that policies should target the least served to expose, address, and uplift them. Strategic inputs then create improvements that cascade outward, affecting the policies and practices of the larger ecosystem.

Similar to powell's theory of change about targeted universalism, Serna contends that the BCLC does not just benefit African Americans. For instance, even

though it focuses on educating Black families about safe sleeping habits for infants, he tells me, "We are pursuing interventions that will help all children."
He continues, "I think everyone's going to have some important takeaways. . . .
The interventions that we develop around child abuse and neglect, homicides,
third-party homicides will probably, most likely, benefit the broader community." He then cites the example of youth gun violence. Most gun violence in
Sacramento is nestled inside particular areas of the city, but Black people are not
the only folks who live and spend time there. "Just because you're white or non-
African American, you're not immune to violence."

I nod my head in agreement and go right into my next question: "What do
you think are the root causes of the disparities that we're seeing?" His answer is
thoughtful: "I think there's a lot of things. I mean, some of it is institutional racism." I ask Supervisor Serna to be more specific. His analysis is grounded in a
clear understanding of interlocking forms of oppression. He delineates that there
are "inequities socioeconomically, inequities when it comes to educational opportunities, inequities in the history of investments in different parts of our community, different stressors when it comes to racism." He takes a moment and
leans back in his chair. It seems he is pondering his answer.

"It's odd, quite frankly, for a non-African American to say it, but I've come
to learn a great deal about it from professionals and people, the PhDs that study
this. I've had some really enlightening conversations with folks who know the
subject matter a lot better than I do." These conversations have led him to a stark
conclusion: "It is much more challenging for African Americans to raise healthy
children." As he shares his insights, a wave of names come over me: Tamir Rice
(12 years old), Trayvon Martin (17 years old), Michael Brown (18 years old), Stephon A. Clark (22 years old), Ahmaud Arbery (25 years old). There are many
contemporary instances of police murdering Black men and women, and when
these bullets hit children and young adults, they hit differently. African American families *do* raise healthy Black children, but this is often despite a deeply
entrenched system of white supremacy designed and nurtured through policies,
practices, and policing that are wedded to anti-Blackness.

With the vision of these unarmed victims stirring in my mind, I push back a
bit on Supervisor Serna. "As someone who *does* represent government," I assert,
"what are some ways that the system is trying to address and eliminate institutionalized racism?" Phil helps connect the dots between collective activism and
institutional responsibility. "You have to remember," he says, that "the death report" and the formation of the Reduction of African American Child Deaths
committee "all happened, interestingly enough, during the infancy of Black Lives
Matter." He describes a type of "serendipity" where "there was a broader realization across the country that racism has by no means evaporated from the

American milieu." He expounds on this point: "The incidents of violence against African Americans . . . thrust this conversation to the forefront: What do we do as local government? What do we do as state government? Now, unfortunately, with the Trump administration, it has become all too prominent an issue. It's inescapable for everyone. And to some degree, that's kind of a good thing because it forces us to talk about it." Phil brings the conversation full circle. "Institutional racism," he attests, "really presents itself in the form of these massive disparities."

Even though inroads have been made and the death toll has significantly decreased, this work is by no means complete. "The nature of what we're trying to tackle" is complicated and not conducive to a quick "mission accomplished" framework, Phil says. Demanding and creating healthy environments where Black children thrive is a process, much more than a destination. Because this is a lifelong quest, we have "to remind everyone, including the media, that we have a long way to go." "Not for a minute," he contends, "do I think that Sacramento County is somehow an outlier and that the disparities based on race are solely a Sacramento County phenomenon."

Serna's advice for other counties and cities is straightforward. Disaggregate data based on race, and do not be afraid of the findings or try to rationalize the disproportionalities. "If it weren't for that data," patterns of inequality would not have been unveiled in such a blatant and concerted way. "That information," he believes, "really sparked some hearty conversations" and "tough questions early on." Serna is in the early stages of drafting legislation that would require all fifty-eight counties in California to collect similar information to gain greater insight into "the environment of child welfare" and lifelong well-being. As James Baldwin (2014, 25) taught, "Not everything that is faced can be changed, but nothing can be changed until it is faced."

According to Phil, "institutional racism is happening everywhere," and that's why each person needs to "engage in the process of your own governance." Democracy functions through advocacy, but people do not have the same access, opportunities, or time to deal with the government. "I know they don't necessarily want to write emails," he quips, "or perhaps even some are afraid of public speaking," and yet that's "absolutely what it takes." He insists, "Politicians come and go. We are only temporary occupants of our offices." Phil wants his constituents to understand that priorities shift, especially when new mayors and supervisors are sitting around the table. Regardless of who is elected, it is "incumbent upon the community to keep this at the forefront." Change, he affirms, "sustains itself from the bottom up." Then he chuckles and looks right at me: "And, quite frankly, keeps it in the discussions every June" throughout the budget negotiation process. "What I don't want to see happen" is that we are forced to get "our budgets balanced on the backs of the good work that happened." Budget cuts to BCLC "would be a travesty."

"I Am Fighting for My Community"

A lot has happened since the initial "death report." As we reflect on the past eight years, I ask Supervisor Serna what he is most proud of. He instantly tells me that "I'm just proud" of all the ways Community Incubator Leads came to "own it . . . and by that, I mean this ought not to be a top-down approach, this ought not to be big government telling the communities where the disparities are the most pronounced how to do everything. This needs to be a set of solutions, a set of interventions that is a little more organic than that . . . derived from a great deal of input from the communities themselves." Solutions and expertise exist among those who "have been *feeling* the disparity" and "*living with the disparity.*"

The more I listen to Phil Serna's convictions and understand his work behind the scenes, the more my appreciation grows for his role as a servant leader in this movement. Yes, he is a politician, but he does not let politics define the possibilities. He strengthens his convictions with clear data, with real and innovative results. Instead of overseeing colonial modes of operation in which the many serve the few, Phil Serna is a Latino leader who exists to serve the people. "I see myself, fundamentally, as someone that's responsible for doing everything I can to try and give voice to those that don't usually have it or have never possessed it or find it difficult to express themselves politically when it's necessary." In terms of the BCLC, Serna is "very grateful that the community has really taken the reins and really identified it as a very, very high priority for themselves." Building on this energy, Serna wants everyone in Sacramento to "become activists in their own right." He is adamant: "People just need to keep in mind that they really hold the power."

I challenge Phil to move from the general to the specific. I ask him to think about a fifteen-year-old African American student whose cousin was recently murdered. *What would you say to that young man? What would you do?* "I'm a Latino politician. I don't know what it feels like to be an African American fifteen-year-old," but I still have "an obligation." He emphasizes that he wants this student to "know that he's not alone. He's got a community behind him; he's got people that care about him. Even if we're not family. Even if we're not friends. Even if we're not the same race. Even if we come from different neighborhoods." Phil wants to convey the importance of a "focused opportunity" and "stress that he's at a fork in the road." Although Supervisor Serna empathizes with the need to grieve ("mourn his cousin's death in his own way"), he wants to immediately "nurture the alternatives." Many people have similar experiences and find ways to "advance their chances of not being the next victim." So, he surmises, while this young man "has a choice, we have an obligation. That's where the magic can happen where you can really change someone's mind about their limited time on this earth." Supervisor Serna speaks in terms of transformation and purpose, cornerstones of his own life.

The work of racial justice is psychological, physical, and spiritual. In many ways, it is embodied long before it is politicized. Supervisor Serna agrees, sharing that the life and legacies of Black children far exceed "some county supervisor who had an epiphany in 2011." Building on his words, I ask what legacy is Phil Serna trying to leave for the Black children of Sacramento. His response is profound: "That they're living longer. . . . It's a pretty simple way to look at it, but that's what, fundamentally, this is all about." He expounds on his point: "It's not a foreign concept. It's one that has been steeped in the civil right movement. And I challenge anyone to tell me there's something more important than our kids. . . . We're talking about life and death."

Our interview draws to a close, and we look into the future. He tilts his head to the left and seems to be peering far into the distance as he says, "I would like to look back in my old age" and see a "new generation of political leadership." With a glisten in his eye, he shares his sincerest hope: "It would be wonderful" though "probably impossible." I lean forward and prod, asking "What would be impossible?" "What if," Phil opens up, "one of the African American young adults" whose life has been impacted and influenced by the Black Child Legacy Campaign becomes a change agent? Somehow, we could trace back to the effort and say, well . . . *that* baby." Although we cannot know whether the babies whose lives were saved through this work will become our next leaders, it certainly seems that we are moving in the right direction.

In our final moments together, I shift the conversation. I probe Supervisor Serna poetically, giving him the beginning of five sentences and asking him to finish them. Without a moment's hesitation, he offers his responses quickly, simply, and purposefully:

> Black childhood . . . *is difficult.*
> Freedom sounds like . . . *a ballot dropping.*
> Black power feels . . . *like equality.*
> I am fighting . . . *for my community.*
> I am fighting against . . . *the harm of my community.*

Serna's piercing words reach into the heart of his commitment to servant leadership. He continues to connect freedom to the political process and power to equality. Many of the community organizers introduced in subsequent chapters take a slightly different approach.

Vantage points shape perspective. In this moment, I am picturing Ms. Jackie, for instance, for whom Blackness is "nothing but greatness." Her conceptualization and reflection on being African American echoes a similar sentiment articulated by Imani Perry (2019, 21–23) in *Breathe: A Letter to My Sons*: "I do not believe the acts of oppressors are my people's shame. For me, that my people became, created, and imagined from a position of unfreedom is a source of deep pride, not shame. . . . There was love and legacy everywhere." While Ms. Jackie and author Imani Perry both assert an asset-based analysis of their identity as glorious and victorious, Supervisor Serna's perception is different. Perhaps his sympathy is a natural inclination because he is not African American. As an onlooker and witness, he believes, "Black childhood is difficult." The distinctions between these outlooks are important and may point to deeper ideological schisms and manifestations.

Consider the initial naming of this effort when it was in the hands of the Blue Ribbon Commission: *Reduction of African American Child Deaths*. Even though this name was a call to arms to reduce deaths, it was formed, informed, and imbued with loss. Policy makers were reinforcing a deficit lens, even as they were seeking answers to this crisis. Fortunately, they soon realized that centering the Black community would lead to new solutions.

These Black leaders also led us to a new name. I cannot help but grin inside my soul when I consider that RAACD is now a community-driven movement called the *Black Child Legacy Campaign*. Language matters, and names often reflect our values, perceptions, and ambitions. While racism is problematic, shameful, inhumane, gruesome, and challenging, Blackness is not. Blackness is legacy, and this sentiment is simultaneously a compass, definition, and destination.

REFERENCES

Baldwin, James. 2014. *James Baldwin: The Last Interview and Other Conversations*. Brooklyn: Melville House.
Perry, Imani. 2019. *Breathe: A Letter to My Sons*. Boston: Beacon Press.
powell, john a. 2009. "Post-Racialism or Targeted Universalism?" *Denver University Law Review* 86: 785–806.

A UNIQUE OPPORTUNITY, A UNIQUE RESPONSIBILITY
President Chet Hewitt

Maisha T. Winn

As I entered Chet Hewitt's office, he informed me right away that his wife had called, and our time together would need a hard stop at 3:00 P.M. so he could pick up one of his sons. "I'm one of eight kids . . . and I was raised by my sisters," shares Chet. My sisters "were always in charge. As I always say to my wife, 'I take instruction very well.'"

Laughter filled Chet's office overlooking the Sacramento River. The entire building housing the Sierra Health Foundation, where he serves as president and CEO, is a study of light. Generous windows throughout reveal why Sacramento is referred to as the "City of Trees," as well as the "River City." When talking to Chet, it is apparent that the Sierra Health Foundation's vision, "A healthful life for Northern Californians," and mission, "To invest in and serve as a catalyst for ideas, partnerships and programs that improve health and quality of life in Northern California," are informed by his love for his family and for his mother, in particular. According to Chet, his "deep appreciation" for his mother is manifested in the foundation's program portfolio: "Some of the things I saw and some of the things that I'm probably most known for saying are really either direct interpretations or reinterpretations of the lessons my mother shared with me."

From Surviving to Thriving

The Black Child Legacy Campaign (BCLC), for example, seeks to reduce the incidence of infant sleep-related death, child abuse, and third-party homicide in Black families. The inclusion of the word "legacy" within its name is strategic and purposeful. Although Black death is often foreshadowed, notions of "Black legacy" are not. Chet understands this. He notes that only six of his eight siblings are still living: "I can recall my mother's response to losing her oldest son to an asthma attack. And the impact was profound on both the siblings but clearly on my mother who, for the rest of her life, would mourn the fact that she buried a child. It was very clear in her mind that it was supposed to be the other way around." Chet goes on to talk about tensions between the "joy" and "pain" of life and his desire to "advance" the former: "It is much easier for me to think about advancing joy and having kids alive and flourish . . . having their families thrive. . . . That comes very easily born of my own experience and interpreting what this means in my professional life." Indeed, scholars argue that Black children and their families want to "do more than survive" and that there must be ways to counter the "survival industrial complex" too many Black children experience (Love 2019).

Through the Sierra Health Foundation, community members meet to strengthen and create legacies for Black families. Chet and his team provide space and structure for engaging deeply in public health issues that affect Northern Californians. Chet sees BCLC as a potential model for the nation and posits, "I know we're a modest-sized foundation . . . but I do think Sacramento is like many jurisdictions that with the will and investment can turn the tide on the national crisis that black maternal and child mortality represents, and so we have a unique opportunity and unique responsibility." In addition to direct programs that specifically benefit Black children and their families, sleeping assessments of infants now conducted in hospitals because of BCLC advocacy efforts help *all* families. "Good policy for Black families is good policy for all families," asserts Chet.

The Art and Science of Negotiation

Chet began his time with Sierra Health in 2008 and has come to be known as an advocate who can engage in the art of negotiation. At times, his ability to negotiate has challenged his relationships with young activists who want to see things move quickly. Chet says, "I'm a big believer in strategy. . . . We have to think about what we're doing and why . . . and that the art of negotiation is not a weakness."

Chet has compelling ideas to share with young people who wish to engage in equity-oriented and justice-seeking work to bolster the well-being of Black communities:

- The enemies of one's prosperity are not the people in their communities.
- Creating a new narrative is possible through one's scholarship, music, and art.
- The change one hopes for and aspires to cannot be done without one's personal involvement.
- Young people have the right to demand that adults in their community act in ways that promote all the above.

Chet speaks passionately of his desire for young people to know that committing violence against their peers or within their communities will not help them. Reminiscent of Jay-Z's plea, "Please don't die over the neighborhood that your momma rentin," Chet encourages youth to instead strive toward ownership themselves. However, Chet has a more expansive but detailed vision than other elders, who simply want youth to pull up their pants and "do better" in situations without providing any obvious path for doing so.

If adults do not demonstrate accountability to children and youth, as well as a positive vision for their futures, youth have a right to demand it, according to Chet. There is historical context for this ideology. Independent Black Institutions established in the later 1960s and early 1970s throughout the United States asserted such norms when public schools were failing Black and Puerto Rican students. The EAST, for example, in Brooklyn, New York, was home to the Uhuru Sasa School, the *Black News* newspaper, and the Black Experience in Sound performance space. Black teachers, parents, and students who grew tired of the New York City United Federation of Teachers broke away to establish African-centered education through which Black educators encouraged youth to hold adults—including their own family members—to high standards when it came to education and miseducation. When listening to Chet talk about young people, one is reminded of the wisdom that comes with long, slow work and, perhaps, the enduring fable of the tortoise and the hare.

"Most Kids Don't Know My Story"

As leader of the Sierra Health Foundation, Chet established a variety of programs: Build.Black., Kings and Queens Basketball, California Funders for Boys and Men of Color, My Brother's Keeper Initiative, and the Positive Youth Justice

Initiative. Chet put in the work and the time. If one were only to see Chet in his sunlit office, one might make certain assumptions about his upbringing. "Most kids don't know my story," shares Chet. "I am one of eight kids from the projects. Grew up in places that had very similar challenges in a different time. [Youth] need their own contemporaries to show them what that can look like and to guide and help shape their potential, their ideas, their own aspirations."

Invoking Harold Melvin and the Blue Note's song, "Wake Up Everybody," Chet shares a line he would repurpose for twenty-first-century educators: "Teachers, teach the truth." He explains that "the niceties in which we try to think about and speak about the history of challenge in this country need to be unpacked in ways that allow the reality of both the impacts and pushback on those practices and policies to be more clearly understood."

One example Chet gave was the 1963 bombing of the 16th Street Baptist Church in Birmingham that killed four African American girls–fourteen-year-olds Addie Mae Collins, Denise McNair, Carole Robertson, and eleven-year-old Cynthia Wesley. Susan Collins, Addie Mae's little sister, survived but was permanently blinded. Chet was recently working with a group of young men unaware of this historical act of racial terror and hatred. My interview with Chet took place in March 2020, just before people of all ages around the globe collectively witnessed George Floyd's final eight minutes and forty-six seconds of life that a community member filmed on a smartphone. This time, the murder was also witnessed by countless young people who were sheltering in place, isolated from peers by the sudden COVID-19-related closures that exacerbated the shameful inequities of the public education system. The names George Floyd, Breonna Taylor, Ahmaud Arbery, and Elijah McClain are likely deeply imprinted on the hearts and minds of those and other youth who had never learned the names of "the four little girls" who were earlier victims of the ongoing pattern of racism and murder in the United States.

Setting the Table

Chet notes that effective responses to historical injustices have been strategic and purposeful: "There was real strategy and thinking. There was a value and a commitment to a cause. There was a willingness to take on risk. And there was a commitment to this notion of agency and voice in the midst of all the chaos that people saw surrounding them." This strategy is evident in the innovation and foresight of Black Lives Matter founders Alicia Garza, Patrise Khan-Cullors, and Opal Tometi, who brilliantly created a decentralized movement that now has chapters throughout the United States. BCLC has similarly created impact and established a network by distributing leadership and resources throughout Sacramento to ensure that communities that have suffered the most are engaged in personalized ways. In keeping with Chet's firm belief that teachers are not found solely in classrooms and schools, BCLC's Community Incubator Leads have a strong presence in many settings across under-resourced Sacramento neighborhoods.

Sacramento mayor Darryl Steinberg credited the progress made in decreasing the number of homicides involving Black youth in Sacramento to the work of Sierra Health Foundation in a 2019 *Sacramento Bee* article. In that same article, Chet talked about the importance of proactive and holistic engagement, "not just waiting for someone to shoot at somebody, that is not the case . . . it really is around the things we know that add additional stress and trauma in their lives, which sometimes cause people to respond in ways that are not healthy for themselves, their families, or their communities."

Although Chet has little interest in garnering accolades for himself, he is keenly interested in the futures of emerging leaders: "At this point in my career, I am adamant about sharing. . . . Getting old is a challenging thing but what really makes it worthwhile is that you acquire a level of wisdom. . . . I want to set up folks [who] are going to be next." Despite all Chet has achieved with Sierra Health programs and fundraising, he is still not satisfied. Expressing concern that progress on racism and racial disparities has not gone far enough during his thirty-five years of committed work, he shares, "I am not as far as I hoped to be at this point. . . . There is still more to be done for communities of color. . . . I think over the last number of years we've actually gone backward."

Chet's ability to look beyond all he has done and toward the work that has yet to be done is perhaps his greatest gift: his temerity and tenacity to desire more for Black people are palpable. You can see in Chet the boy in a family of eight, wrapped in the love of older siblings and a mother who protected and guided him along the way so he might be of service to others. Chet is a constant gardener; he never lets up and is consistent in his mission to problem solve on behalf of those who need it: "I don't know everything. I don't have the answers to everything, and I always come to the work with a willingness to listen and learn. I think that's what makes you a really good advocate because it's the integration of the best ideas that allows you to have the best chance for success." This gardening is not a form of missionizing or colonizing but is made possible by an intentional leveraging of resources, experience, knowledge, and his own innate ability to facilitate dialogue. Using the metaphor of gumbo, a dish created in Louisiana that varies in terms of the ingredients but always begins with the foundational roux, he explains, "I've always said to folks, it's like making good gumbo, you know. . . . It ain't one thing . . . and you know gumbo can have several people cooking it from the same ingredients and it ain't all gonna be the same. Some folks, maybe they should fry the chicken [laughter], but you leave those experiences with an appreciation of what other people can bring to the table. And it doesn't have to minimize what you have to offer at all."

Setting the table so that others may bring their offerings defines another truth about Chet's leadership: "Leadership is like love. [There's] no shortage of a need for it to be present."

REFERENCES

Jay-Z. 2017. "The Story of O.J." *4:44*. Roc Nation.

Love, B. 2019. *We Want to Do More than Survive: Abolitionist Teaching and the Pursuit of Educational Freedom*. Boston: Beacon Press.

Sullivan, M. 2020. "Teen Homicides Fall to Zero as Sacramento Sees Overall Decline in Murders in 2019." *Sacramento Bee*, January 28. https://www.sacbee.com/news/local/crime/article239093098.html.

MOTHERING FOR TRANSFORMATION

Kindra Montgomery-Block

Vanessa Segundo

On March 19, 2020, exactly ten days before the mandatory state lockdown announced by Governor Gavin Newsom, I met with Kindra Montgomery. The realness of COVID-19 began to sink deeper and deeper into my body, mind, and spirit. I was five months pregnant at that point, and all I could think about was my son, who moved and kicked inside my womb, not knowing how best to prepare to protect him in what quickly became a global pandemic. I sang to him. I rubbed my belly. I prayed over him.

> The anxiety and isolation many have felt during the past few months while staying at home to prevent community spread of COVID-19 is a peek into the uncertainty and fear Black communities face daily.
>
> —Kindra Montgomery-Block

Later, Kindra shared this wisdom with me, noting that the COVID-19 pandemic revealed how states had to make the decision either to "prioritize the health of residents" or "the health of the economy." This decision underscores the values that sustain the various systems of inequities that not only harm but also persecute Black communities. What is worth saving? Who is considered worthy enough to save? Who is making this decision?

Legacy Begins at the West End of Louisville, Kentucky

I first met Kindra during meetings with the Sierra Health Foundation when I not only learned about the Black Child Legacy Campaign but also came to understand her leadership role. As associate director of community and economic development for the foundation, Kindra spent the past six years spearheading the creation of the Community Incubator Lead model that forms the foundation of BCLC programming. Kindra has been instrumental in creating personalized programs for communities around workforce training, job placement, counseling, maternal health, infant and child health, and county services. Her involvement in dimensions of evaluation, planning, and execution is underscored by her fervor to center and uplift community partnerships. She is in the business of forming and sustaining relationships. It is no coincidence that Kindra played a central role in BCLC's ability to surpass a 2020 goal of reducing Black child deaths by 33 percent in a five-year timeframe while securing financial investments totaling $10.9 million for capacity building across the seven communities engaged in this initiative. These are the same communities Kindra and her family belong to; these are places and people who have raised her, mentored her, loved her. I am eager to learn more.

I make the fifteen-minute drive to the Sierra Health Foundation, deciding to take the side streets that day to enjoy the spring breeze and sunlight that entered through my car windows, bringing with them the smell of the newly blossomed flowers and trees that lined Arden Way. I let the calmness of the Sacramento River guide me to my destination. Although it was not my first time visiting the foundation, the picturesque foliage and sound of the gentle river waves surrounded me as if it were our first encounter. The beautifully manicured bushes and lawn hugged the three-story modern building and its gradated beige-to-brown brickwork. I pulled into the visitor parking spot right across from the main entrance and took a few minutes to stand outside before entering, taking in the calmness and silence that seemed to permeate the entire building. I made my way up to the second floor via the half-spiraled wooden staircase that led me to our meeting location, a small conference room; there I sat in an executive chair, one of six that framed the medium-sized oval table. Kindra's presence immediately added life to the space, as energy radiated in her words she uses to describe her work at that moment.

As she breathed her full name into existence, the empty walls became adorned with the images of the women who are part of her maternal and paternal lineage, who guided and uplifted Kindra in the important work of "loving Black mommies."

Kindra. Inspired by Hurricane Kendra, Kindra's mother wanted to name her daughter with a unique moniker. Indeed, the decision to select a name from the last season in history to use an all-female Atlantic hurricane naming list manifested her expectation that, like the two key features of the related natural phenomenon, Kindra would have a path and strength that were not undermined but instead forecasted for their power.

Hurricane Kendra, which touched ground in Puerto Rico on October 28, 1978, soon became a tropical storm that lasted for a week, producing heavy rains and damage upward of six million dollars. Exactly thirty years later to the day, Kindra gave birth to her first child Samone; she also marked her first month as the program officer overseeing the Steering Committee on Reduction of African American Child Deaths and its groundbreaking work that lay the foundation for the BCLC. Earlier Kindra had served as director of training and community relations for the Center for Community School Partnerships of the School of Education at the University of California, Davis. Her twenty years of experience strengthening the capacity of community-based organizations reinforced Kindra's commitment to "civic duty and a need to improve the lives of youth and families."

Kindra's middle name is Frances which is an acknowledgment of her paternal great-grandmother's embodiment of the legacy of mothering for transformation. A Black woman, Great-Grandmother Frances defiantly married a white man and raised twelve sons and one daughter, despite the racism and targeted discrimination they experienced. One of her daughters was Kindra's great-aunt Georgia, a politician and celebrated civil rights pioneer. During her twenty-one-year tenure as the first Black senator in the state of Kentucky, Great-Aunt Georgia Montgomery Davis Powers sponsored legislation prohibiting sex, job, and age discrimination while also introducing the first statewide fair housing laws. Kindra's admiration for her kinswoman instills a sense of pride in her; her great-aunt also represents a standard of advocacy to "hold my head up high about this work."

Kindra understands the level of commitment and sacrifice that Great-Aunt Georgia made to navigate the racist Kentucky legislature and is reminded that there are no excuses not to do the work. Even though her Kentucky family often draws comparisons between Great-Aunt Georgia and herself as two "spitfires," Kindra chooses to honor the role of Great-Grandmother Frances in raising "this great Black woman" who engaged in acts of "reimaging a future where Black lives flourish and thrive in their totality."

Kindra's mother, an attorney for the agency that was formerly the Department of Mental Health Services in Sacramento, came from a family of doctors and educators who were compelled to serve and advocate for Black communities.

Collectively, they set the expectation that you give back and contribute something to this world.

Montgomery Block. The Montgomerys are a household name in Louisville, known for their significant contributions to Black life and activism. Kindra recalls Black excellence as central to their advocacy work. It was no surprise to learn that they mentored youth and instilled a commitment to fight for the future of their community. Kindra's father and two sisters grew up next to professional boxer, philanthropist, and social activist Muhammad Ali, a close family friend. In fact, Kindra's grandfather gave Muhammad Ali his first job, working alongside the Montgomerys. Kindra's married name, Block, represents a similar legacy of community activism in Sacramento, where Uncle Harry Block was caringly referred to as the mayor of Del Paso Heights. Becoming part of the Block family amplified Kindra's ability to cultivate strong community ties and sustain relationships with Black families who rightly distrust government-sponsored support services. This lineage is the backdrop to Kindra being "not just the pushy Black girl from Valley High" but a public steward from and within the community.

Motherwork as Leadership, Activism, and Liberation

The undeniable connection between becoming a Black mother and serving mothers is woven into Kindra's work and life. "My story is for Samone," she tells me.

An expectant mom myself, I ask Kindra about what her experience was like to birth her first child and BCLC at the same time. Kindra had exactly one month to plan a strategic blueprint for the initial phases of the work while embodying what it is and means to be a Black mother. She was living with all the tensions and possibilities of Black maternal health while unraveling and unveiling the deeply rooted systemic issues of oppression, injustice, and inequity systemized through practices and policies within and beyond the health sector. She tells me, "You have to make sure you have the right cortisol in your body." I was taken aback by this response. Cortisol, a steroid hormone produced by the adrenal glands, has several functions but mainly assists the body in responding to stress or danger, often referred to as our fight or flight response. Recent studies show a direct connection between unbalanced levels of maternal cortisol and neuropsychiatric disorders. Kindra seems to read my mind and satisfies my curiosity: "Cortisol. That hormone is about love. It's about justice. It's about producing the best human that you can. How can you do that if everything else around you is on fire?" My baby kicks. We both sit with what Kindra offers, in silence.

After a moment, Kindra says, "Throughout this journey, no one ever said, 'I love Black moms.'" As we both stare at each other, I know we both understand what her statement means, in all its dimensions and forms.

It is unforgivable to focus on infant and child mortality without acknowledging the persecution of Black women in American society, given their disproportionate experiences of violence, rape, homicide, police brutality, incarceration, and institutionalized racism. "No one ever says, I love Black mommies. I do." As tears enter our space, we both honor the depth and truth of her words. Kindra's work is not only about building the capacity of community organizations to empower Black children and youth to thrive but also about creating justice-centered futures where Black mothers are protected and sacred.

"Our bodies are on fire. Our environment's on fire so we can't have healthy babies all the time. Someone has to love us enough to speak about it," Kindra says. She asks if I was expecting my first child, and I respond that I am carrying my second beautiful brown baby. "Then you know. You understand," she replies.

At that moment, I no longer am in a meeting space but am transported to the last month of Kindra's pregnancy, when she received the call from Sierra Health Foundation to "work on saving Black kids' lives" while preparing to have a Black child of her own. Kindra spent her entire life preparing for that particular call, a call to help "the Black community strategize with system leaders" to "lift and love Black people." Growing up in South Sacramento, Kindra tells me that her pride in being a Valley High School graduate was at the root of her interest in studying political science at the University of California, Riverside; there, she worked at a nonprofit organization that developed substance abuse intervention and prevention programs for youth. Inspired by this experience, she worked for several years at the Youth Leadership Institute in San Francisco after graduation. On completing her master's degree in public administration from Golden Gate University, Kindra returned to her hometown Sacramento to work for ten years at the University of California, Davis. School of Education. Collectively, these experiences reinforced her commitment to community-led advocacy efforts for equity and justice.

I was transported to her short-lived maternity leave, a time when she celebrated the growth in her family while negotiating health equity initiatives that centered Black families at an institutional level. Kindra was nine months pregnant when she joined Sierra Health Foundation. Thirty days after her start date, she was initiating her recovery from a high-risk pregnancy while simultaneously preparing to return to her leadership role overseeing the Steering Committee on Reduction of African American Child Deaths. Shifting from self and baby care to prioritizing community needs meant that personal sacrifices needed to be made—another reason Kindra deems it important to ensure that the work culture she is part of normalizes motherhood.

At the core of Kindra's work is the celebration of Black mothers: "It's not that I don't love all mommies. It's kind of like the Black Lives Matter conversation." I am intrigued and asks her to tell me more. She replies, "My house matters. Your house matters. But my house is on fire. We have to do immediate things to focus on that house because if we don't, then it's going to spread to your house and spread to your neighborhood." BCLC represented an opportunity to create equity transformation in health systems, particularly in communities that are home spaces for Kindra. Reflecting on more than twenty years of community organizing, she notes that most of her time has been dedicated to prevention work that did not focus on interrogating, building, and protecting infrastructures and economic investments that positively affect Black communities. "Now is an opportunity to think ahead, to strategize," says Kindra.

Kindra points to the window at the corner of the room in which we are seated and begins to describe the economic development funds being poured into downtown Sacramento. The skyline is framed by new high rises, condominiums, and gated communities; continuing roadwork improvements; and renovations to the city landscape. Kindra describes how the concentration of economic investments in white neighborhoods signals the inequitable distribution of wealth and the maintenance of poverty in neighborhoods where predominantly low-income folks of color reside. Take, for instance, Meadowview, the community where Kindra played softball as a youth, which continues to look like the place she visited in the 1990s when "not a spotlight or pothole is being fixed." BCLC has demonstrated pathways to inclusive economic development through direct investments into Black communities that positively influence the welfare not only of children but also of entire family units. In essence, BCLC represents "Build.Black."—infrastructure by which to bring to the fore issues of inequity experienced by Black communities "like never before, without impunity."

I am also transported to the many meetings Kindra held with various stakeholders across the state and country who expressed varied beliefs about whether BCLC would be successful. She recalls the first meeting with the Board County Supervisors, where she coordinated the participation of various community organizations in demanding funding and resources that represented reinvestment into defunded neighborhoods: "They said to elected officials, not only are we going to be able to take on this challenge, we're going to be the ones to fix it." Indeed, community partnerships are the heart of BCLC and are leveraged to amplify preexisting efforts. The resulting success of this solidarity work has been rightfully celebrated and acknowledged. It was no surprise that several of the organizations and stakeholders who were once on the sidelines and skeptical about the work later publicly claimed ownership and credit of this movement. Kindra, always intentional and strategic, knows the significance of this self-proclaimed involvement: "The more people that own it, then they really got to own it. We can find a spot for you too." She is not interested in who wants to take credit for reaching benchmarks, but only in those invested in these neighborhoods to ensure that Black communities "actually stay alive and thrive."

I am transported to community circles where the work of building Black futures is rooted and protected. Kindra had shared with me the reports her team created that describe the benchmarks and the associated quantitative datasets that confirm the success of their work. I ask her to speak more about what she considers the most significant lesson her community partners taught her. She takes a deep breath. Inhales. Exhale. "It's the opportunity to save Black lives," she answers. Another deep breath. Inhales. Exhales.

The killing of Stephon Clark, an unarmed Black youth, by the Sacramento police on Sunday, March 18, 2018, represented a pivotal moment for Kindra in her roles as part of BCLC and as a Black mother in Sacramento. "When something so tragic like this happens, it takes the soul out of the neighborhood," she reflects. All the accolades directed at BCLC programming seemed small as the realities of "picking Black people off the cement or burying a Black person" sink in. No benchmark or data point could revive Stephon. No recognition could ease the pain of Stephon Clark's mother grieving the loss of her son, like so many Black mothers had done before her.

Kindra says, "Stephon Clark's murder served as a reminder that our unprecedented results were insufficient and insignificant at the same time." Caught between her role as a community activist and an activist from the community, Kindra saw the tragedy as both personal and professional; she had grown up and had direct relationships with the families affected. She says, "These families that I had grown up around my whole life did not have a way to create an opportunity for that generation to thrive. It wasn't about services or better resources." Compelled to strengthen the solidarity among the "Black civil rights infrastructure in Sacramento," Kindra organized a gathering of key Black stakeholders and organizations to work toward a unified voice that not only responded to the state of violence against Black bodies in Sacramento but also planned for the future of Black Sacramento. Birthed from this gathering was the "idea around inclusive economic development," infrastructure, and systems designed to create long-term investments in all aspects of life in Black communities that became Build.Black. More than an economic strategy to reduce poverty, it was a strategy to redistribute wealth in communities that had systemically and historically been denied resources. It was no coincidence that these communities were the seven neighborhoods that were part of BCLC. The true work lies in helping these communities heal.

The true work also lies in empowering the community by leveraging their knowledge and assets to reimagine futures that are in the "active pursuit of justice." I feel compelled to ask her thoughts about a proverb triggered by her reflection: until the lion learns how to write, every story will glorify the hunter. Kindra responds, "Figure out how to write like a lion. Honestly, we're not speaking the right language or writing the right language." Kindra has been writing in lion; in fact, she has mastered it. As a systems leader, Kindra advocates for Black communities to assert themselves for themselves.

Kindra's passion is guided by an unwavering commitment to facilitate capacity building to create and build futures for Black communities, humanizing Black lives through the process. Kindra's advocacy does not end when she walks out of her office or when the clock strikes five. Having interacted with colleagues from the multiple spheres that Kindra navigates, I know she is highly involved in various initiatives, community boards, and other activities. In admiration, I ask how she sustains herself. "Through the grace of God," she replies simply.

She tells me her faith is central to grounding her work and word. Her husband and daughter are constant sources of support and joy. The genuine smile that sweeps across her face is one of pure happiness when she describes Baron, the new puppy they gave to Samone. Time with her family is "protected time": nothing interrupts Kindra's role as mother and wife. She also describes her circle of "sister soldiers and mentors" as a consistent source of empowerment to all dimensions of her being; they are people with whom she has no need to compartmentalize herself, because they see her for who she truly is. She explains, "We do what women do, lift each other up." They help her strategize and maintain clarity about the real work that needs to be accomplished in the community.

As I stare at Kindra, I can feel the depth of her genuine commitment to do right by the community that raised and mentored her. Her energy transmits an unwavering life mission to continue the work of "celebrating Black folks' lives." I am interested in learning what she considers BCLC's biggest success. Rather than referring to a data point or describing a personal victory, Kindra insists that the true significance of the work is its ability to amplify preexisting community initiatives created by and for Black families and to reaffirm their role in creating transformative change. "I want Black communities to know that they are powerful," she says with conviction. In poetic prose, she declares forcefully:

> Black childhood is . . . *necessary.*
> Black power feels like . . . *self-love.*
> When I look into our past, I . . . *see our future.*
> When I look in the mirror, I . . . *see Samone.*

THE PRESIDENT OF HELPING AND GIVING

Crystal Harding

Lawrence "Torry" Winn

Sitting at her desk several feet away from the workspaces of her Black Child Legacy Campaign colleagues, Crystal juggles her time, answering phone calls, troubleshooting with staff, and preparing for an upcoming activity with teens from Foothill High School and Highlands High School. "We have a teen event in a few hours that we are getting ready for. We try to make them feel welcome and for them to know they matter," she says, referring to the Youth Participatory Action Research (YPAR) program associated with BCLC. She continues to talk about the event and urges me to stay to participate or, as she suggests, "observe the teens in action."

As Crystal is sharing the logistics, details, and purpose of the teen event, a young African American woman opens the door, positions herself in the middle of the entryway, and requests a few minutes of Crystal's time. Crystal lets me know that this will only take a moment. She quickly steps away, walks toward the woman, and listens closely to her concerns.

As they are talking, I want to give them their privacy to discuss the issue at hand and slowly stand up to look around the large office. This is my second visit to a BCLC office, so I am curious to see differences in its layout and decoration. I count five work desks. I see two other people whom I have yet to be introduced to. They are immersed in a conversation but acknowledge my presence with a gentle wave. In one corner of the office, literature is neatly placed on a table and posted on a wall. I begin to drift off wondering: Who works in the office with Crystal? How often do visitors come into the space for help? Do all BCLC offices look the same with neatly decorated collateral material? How do the different agencies coordinate their schedules or share data? Who is responsible for communications?

The woman, who needed a hot-quick second with Crystal, now seems reassured by Crystal's confidence in her. She thanks Crystal, then dashes down the hallway, and disappears. I look at Crystal and laugh, saying, "Real time, real-time needs." With a smile, she also laughs and nods, "My goodness!" Translation: there is a lot going on here today but "it's gonna be alright." Now we are both laughing. This moment of humor, laughter, and optimism is what the entire hour and a half with Crystal feels like.

Crystal's gift to respond with grace and patience to a series of urgencies is just one of the qualities required to be successful in meeting the needs of others. Getting back on task after being interrupted is a talent. Shifting from answering the telephones to responding to emails, from sending off texts to sitting down for an interview, from giving someone just a minute of your time to giving them an hour can be exhausting for many. But for Crystal—and many of her Community Lead Incubator (CIL) colleagues—juggling roles, coordinating community events, meeting with clients and partners, supervising volunteers, inputting data, writing reports, applying for grants, responding to injustices, completing assigned deliverables, and remaining positive are necessary components of her effectiveness.

I am curious about her job description, how she manages to get it all done, and why she is committed to serving the Black community of Sacramento. I also want to know how she remains motivated and positive. These daily tasks and impromptu meetings (as well as sporadic emergencies) are all parts of Crystal's lifetime goal to help people, work with youth, and collaborate with others to improve the quality of life for marginalized communities of color.

Within just a few minutes of meeting her, it is evident that she has the capacity and competence to comfort others who are in dire need and reassurance of "it's gonna be alright." She exudes a sense of confidence that rubs off on the individuals she encounters. Crystal, like many of her CIL peers, is very experienced and skilled: she is a valuable and integral member of the Sacramento community.

A 10,000-Mile Journey of Liberation and Hope

As the program director for the North Highlands Foothill Farms Black Child Legacy Campaign, Crystal finds herself fulfilling her dream as a social worker.

She and the supporting agencies for the Community Incubator Leads dedicate their time and resources to the local youth and families of North Highlands, Foothill Farms, and surrounding neighborhoods. Their purpose is clear: "to serve as a conduit connecting people to power. Let them know that we are here for them. We can hold their hands and walk with them along the way." Her walk with others during challenging times and her steady hand in moments of uncertainty are deeply rooted in her life journey—literally encompassing more than ten thousand miles—and the lessons she learned along the way.

Crystal's zealous fight for families begins seven thousand miles away from Sacramento. As a child she and her family resided in Liberia. Located in Western Africa on the Atlantic Ocean, Liberia was founded in 1822 by freed American and Caribbean slaves (Americo Liberians). It is Africa's oldest republic. When Crystal was seven years old, a civil war broke out, which ultimately killed more than 250,000 people and destroyed many homes, businesses, and infrastructure. It also forced Crystal and her family to leave Liberia and make the journey to Oakland, California, in the early 1990s. After residing in the Bay Area for a few years, in 1994 her family moved another one hundred miles east to Sacramento where the cost of living and employment opportunities were more advantageous.

On graduating from Foothill High School, she journeyed another 2,300 miles to Montgomery, Alabama, to attend Alabama State University (ASU), a historically black college and university (HBCU). Montgomery is the home of Rosa Parks and where the 1955–1956 boycott of public buses helped elevate the civil rights movement to a national and global level. It is the place where Dr. Martin Luther King Jr. pastored Dexter Avenue Baptist Church. ASU is situated within the heart of America's freedom movement and the fight for the recognition that Black lives matter. Crystal's educational experience at an HBCU gave her insight into race and social justice issues. She began to grapple with the impacts of colorism, anti-Blackness, and the oppression of Black, Indigenous, and People of Color (BIPOC). More importantly, she was surrounded by a community of Black students and professors, which felt very similar to her experiences in her native country of Liberia where Black African culture, thought, and life were celebrated. After graduating with a BA degree in social work, she then traveled another 2,300 miles back to Sacramento, where she received her MSW degree from Sacramento State University before working for several nonprofits in the region.

Crystal first learned about BCLC when invited by the Liberty Towers CIL to attend a Profound Purpose Institute. The institute provides a powerful structure of support for CILs, the Steering Committee, and other community leaders to build collaborative relationships and a learning community. In the fall of 2018, the North Highlands Foothill Farms incubator hired her as the program director, and her dream as a social worker came to fruition: "When I was younger, I told people that my dream job was to be president of helping and giving. I did not know that was social work and philanthropy." As the program director, she feels right at home advocating, creating innovative solutions, helping, and working with community members. She is applying the lessons learned from her journey of ten thousand miles—responding to the needs of the community where she grew up, currently lives, works, prays, and plays.

A Celebration of Life

Crystal shares her workspace with the members of the North Highlands Foothill Farms multidisciplinary team. Standing up from her desk, she points out where her team members work during the day. But before she is able to provide the details of the office space, the phone rings, and we both laugh again at her "real-time" requests. She finishes her call and then points out that one desk is reserved for a representative from the Department of Human Assistance (DHA); another one is for a Child Protective Services (CPS) employee. The last desk area is for the Probation Team. She introduces me to the DHA employee. The middle-aged woman describes her work and the collaborative efforts between the different agencies. She points out that she has already witnessed success in the community and that Black lives are being saved and their needs are being met. Crystal later shares a passionate description of the multidisciplinary team: "We meet the families as they are. Connecting with them. No judgment. Just open arms and open hearts. And with genuine love and empathy, so that they know they have someone, a team, and network that's there to support them through it all."

The team works together to ensure that families do not fall between the cracks and do not miss out on any opportunities or resources. Crystal makes it clear that programming, resources, staffing, and the name itself of BCLC are important but that "a personal story or personal connection" makes it relatable for the community. Crystal's natural gift to relate and show compassion for the concerns and needs of others makes it easier for community members to trust her. Trust is essential to building healthy relationships with vulnerable families, many of whom are skeptical of government agencies or nonprofits because of failed promises.

The role of the program director is not just connecting the family to resources and helping individuals figure out urgent issues. "We are here to celebrate with them," asserts Crystal. This is evident in the abundance of love and support that the youth of North Highlands Foothill Farms receive throughout the year. After visiting with Crystal, I received an email inviting me to a February 2019 Student Voices gathering. Local leaders, elected officials, law enforcement, school administrators, and community service providers came to this gathering to listen to the youth and the incredible insight they bring to "the table." According to Crystal, "the youth are the why. They are our present and future, we are doing this work for their generation to thrive and really live fully. We need to start engaging and connecting with them when they are younger. We will be able to have greater impact partnering with them." I still receive an email every two months from Crystal highlighting and celebrating the progress and achievements of young people.

Black Beauty, Liberation, and Education

Several posters with positive and uplifting sayings and images of Black youth and families decorate the walls of the North Highlands Foothill Farms BCLC office. They are neatly displayed on a table and perfectly angled on a wall. I am drawn near by the big green words "BLACK CHILD LEGACY CAMPAIGN" spread across every piece of literature. This small space dedicated to BCLC literature, news, and information feels sacred. The images of Black families and black excellence featured on the collateral material bring joy to Crystal. As a native of a country that was the first republic in Africa and was founded by freed enslaved people from the United States and the Caribbean, she appreciates Black beauty, liberation, education, and self-determination. Crystal did not always see these images and language of Black empowerment in Sacramento.

As a child and later as a young adult, she experienced the impact of the media's negative portrayal of Black people and the agonizing pains of colorism. "Being darker skinned and not seeing us on TV all the time or teachers not reflecting my culture or respecting my difference" frustrated her. Crystal speaks adamantly about the way Black children are represented in school textbooks and in the media. The great histories of Black legacies are not accurately described; even worse, they are most often invisible or left out of the K–12 curriculum. When Black children only see anti-Blackness themes and negative images of them and their communities, they internalize them. She expresses how schools and the media perpetuate these harms and lower the self-esteem of many Black students, especially Black girls. "What are we teaching our babies? Our Black babies?" asks Crystal.

In addition to the pervasiveness of anti-Blackness, white supremacy, and cultural imperialism in K–12 schools and the influence of negative media depictions, Crystal also deals with the issue of colorism, which is when light-skinned individuals are given preferential treatment over darker-skinned individuals. Every ethnic group (Latinx, Asian, etc.) struggles with colorism. Crystal recalls attending Alabama State University and learning about African American history and discussing the impacts of colorism. It was one of her first times she felt liberated and connected to others who thought like her. BCLC provides a similar space and platform for her and others to talk about the mistreatment and dehumanization of Black folk because of the color of their skin. She embraces the name "Black Child Legacy Campaign" because it elevates Black people and highlights their past and their future. It also gives hope to young people in elementary, high school, and college to see themselves as leaders in their community. CIL staff and other BCLC leaders are present in the community, working with apartment complexes, schools and their staff and students, community-based organizations, and partner agencies. The constant promotion of the name "Black Child Legacy Campaign" and the appearance of Black leaders speaking positively and eloquently not only about the issues in the Black community but also about successes and accomplishments push back against the deficit model narrative of Black people. She believes that BCLC helps shape a positive narrative. BCLC leaders provide black youth with positive role models and examples of Black people changing the world.

Futures Matter

Crystal leads me down one of the hallways of Liberty Towers Church, which is the site of the North Highlands Foothill Farms BCLC local office. It is located about fifteen minutes north of downtown Sacramento off I-80. We enter a room that is bustling with teens. The students are preparing to participate in Student Voices, one of the youth programs affiliated with BCLC, which uses YPAR to engage students to change their community.

Student Voices is one of the emerging success stories of the North Highlands Foothill Farm BCLC. It connects local high school students with local leaders, elected or appointed officials, and service providers. However, the youth are the trusted experts in charge. This program provides a "brave space" and time for students to let their voices be heard and share their concerns, ideas, solutions, and perspective on the present and future. In the process, they provide authentic recommendations to policy makers. The intergenerational attendees share their hopes for their community. Student Voices is one effective way that the Liberty Towers CIL engages youth to reduce Black child deaths. BCLC's work is not always about reviewing data or participating in protests, but about finding ways for "them to use their voices, provide solutions, discuss their fears, and to actively collaborate for brighter futures." The goal is to collectively amplify teen voices and implement their suggestions without red tape.

Crystal stands back from the YPAR Circle and watches the youth with a proud smile. They are lively, bubbly, talkative, and engaged. Crystal continues to smile. She knows that the future is bright, and this is why *we gonna be alright*.

REVOLUTIONARY RELATIONS

Jackie Rose

Vajra M. Watson

The Rose Family Creative Empowerment Center (RFCE) is located at 2251 Florin Road inside the Sojourner Truth African Heritage Museum. RFCE was founded as a nonprofit organization in 2013 and has expanded steadily since then. Through a variety of roles and capacities, its staff have been serving the South Sacramento area for nearly three decades.

Sacramento is known as the "City of Trees" because of the dense diversity of elms, oaks, and sycamores (to name a few) that cover nearly one-quarter of the urban landscape. It is in the fall of 2018 that I make my way from my home on the Northside, along I-5 South, into the Meadowview neighborhood to meet with the center's founder and executive director, Jackie Rose. This time of year is especially colorful as leaves are changing colors and dancing toward the ground. Today the air is brisk, and the sky is an aqua blue with scattered white clouds on the horizon. This picturesque backdrop surrounds me.

I exit on Florin Road East, make a left on 24th, and pass the Chevron on the left and California Bank and Trust on the right before making my way into the large parking lot of an array of storefronts like Mi Rancho Grocery and Boost Mobile. Amidst this array of buildings is an established community hub that houses artwork and various social services. As soon as I enter through the tinted-glass doors, I am greeted by a large mural high on the wall depicting local African American heroes and sheroes of Sacramento, among them Cornel West. The space feels historic and welcoming. I am eager to find Ms. Jackie.

I go down a dim hallway, make a left, and see a sign with green, black, and white lettering announcing the Black Child Legacy Campaign. I know I am in the right place. After talking to a few staff members, I wait for Ms. Jackie in the conference room. Inside this room, the walls are full of images of Black excellence. There is a framed poster of Coretta Scott King and another of President Barack Obama, Reverend Martin Luther King Jr., and Rosa Parks with this caption: "Rosa Parks sat so King could walk; Obama ran so that our children might fly."

History Matters

Ms. Jackie has deep roots in Sacramento, and these roots have shaped her understanding of leadership and social change. She begins by proudly telling me, "I was born and raised here in Sacramento." Ms. Jackie grew up in the Del Paso Heights neighborhood and emphasizes that it was a "community village." Much of Ms. Jackie's work now revolves around reclaiming and rebuilding this sense of a village. And even though she has spent the latter part of her professional career working in Meadowview, her most profound life lessons came from the homegrown "village of elders" that nurtured her development as an adolescent. "That was in the 70s with bell bottoms and platform shoes," she tells me as she flashes a wide smile, winks, and seems to know she doesn't quite look her age. Then, rather abruptly, her facial expression changes, and her posture straightens when I ask about some of her most influential mentors. In the community that raised her, one man stands out: *Mr. Echols.*

Mr. Echols was the custodian at Grant High School, "a gentleman that only had a sixth-grade education." He was originally from the South and had a distinct southern accent. "He would always talk very slow but the words that he would leave you with would be so profound." When Ms. Jackie was in high school, she could always turn to Mr. Echols for advice. Even as an adult, he continued to encourage her to get involved in the community.

She quickly provides an example. Years ago, when her son's Little League team was in turmoil, Mr. Echols told her to join its board. Following his advice, Ms. Jackie became vice president at a time when it was "pretty much male dominated. I thought my interest was just my son at the time," she remembers, "but it wasn't really just my son—it was all those kids. It was hundreds of kids that were part of that 'cause sports is a big deal in Del Paso Heights." Ms. Jackie helped the league become financially solvent and better organized. And then right when she was contemplating leaving the board because it was "pretty stable" and she wanted to "kinda just play a mother's role," Mr. Echols told her, quite frankly, "It's not time for you to do that." Again, he played a pivotal role, convincing her to coach her son's senior league team. She laughs as she remembers his directive: "You gotta go coach." Ms. Jackie pushed back and told him, "I don't know nothing about baseball." But he was insistent: "You sat on the benches long enough. You know a little bit about, you know, baseball." After some trepidation, Ms. Jackie recalls, "I became the coach." Mr. Echols had that way of making an impact. When Ms. Jackie stepped into that role of baseball coach, it "really opened the door up for a lot of women in Del Paso Heights to [gain] leadership roles that were male dominated."

This example provides a glimpse into the ways she was mentored, sometimes with a little tough love and nudging. Mr. Echols shaped Ms. Jackie's trajectory of service, but he was not the only one. She speaks seriously about the ways adults surrounded her with an ethic of care, critical consciousness, and consistency. When asked what exactly this village taught her, she precisely narrows it down to four components: "The first thing they taught me is to watch and listen to them. You needed to sit at the table, really hear what they were saying, how they were saying it, and what was being said. I think there's a lot to be said for just sitting back and watching someone."

Second, at a relatively young age, Ms. Jackie accompanied community leaders to neighborhood association meetings and city council convenings. In these spaces, she learned a valuable second lesson: "watching them come to those meetings very organized, very systematically, with an agenda of items that they wanted to see changed or they wanted to make sure that the entire community was informed about."

The third component she learned is to be "really intentional about this work." She repeats, "Really being intentional. Being intentional about picking your battles and not getting caught up in the small stuff that wasn't going to be impactful. And so, I learned that from them."

Finally, Ms. Jackie witnessed the ways the adults in her life interacted and had very "strong relationships with the community." She explains that "relationship building" is paramount, especially with families who have been systematically disenfranchised. To disrupt cycles of hopelessness and marginalization, genuine trust must be forged. That is the only way "they [will] feel comfortable that you are their advocate" and "that you are going to serve them."

Growing up in Del Paso Heights, Ms. Jackie was taught about the importance of observation, discernment, intentionality, and activism. These are cornerstones of her lifelong work, and she remains a consistent force for change throughout Sacramento because of them.

Intergenerational Justice

For the last thirty years, Ms. Jackie has been supporting families in South Sacramento. In the late 1990s, she worked for a development agency that was managing an infamous apartment complex called by many names: G-Parkway, Jean Parkway, Franklin Villa, or Phoenix Park. Although that area has since improved "one family at a time" by making sure people are "connected to social services," other pockets of Sacramento are still painfully marginalized. She brings up Providence Place Apartments in the Valley High area where she is currently working to disrupt those "same patterns of poverty. Same patterns of hopelessness. Same patterns of crime. We have a model that we used in Phoenix Park," she explains, "where it doesn't have to be that way." She is adamant: "We must make sure that we serve those people in a way that is gonna be supportive of them in a very dignified way."

The word "dignified" creates a pause between us. Ms. Jackie has discovered that many people who work with the most disenfranchised populations provide a horrifically low quality of services—and get away with it. She explains that families do have challenges, but it's "still my job to make sure that I service them at the highest level." This is something Ms. Jackie is known for throughout Sacramento, and people often tell her, "I know you don't do no junk."

"The dignity that people come to the table with," she asserts, "gets lost in the traditional service delivery model." "These institutions"—she shakes her head as she provides an example—"where you have to sit out in the lobby for two or three hours at a time with four or five kids just waiting for an appointment." The institutional apparatus foresakes the humanity and it "don't work." Even services delivered with the best intentions can strip people of their dignity. And then, logically, folks do not want to come back. "So who loses in that?" Ms. Jackie asks rhetorically. "The babies I love so dearly lose in that" because of the lack of common decency and basic respect.

As an alternative, Ms. Jackie's approach centralizes relationships. She creates spaces for a connection to unfold where "barriers are broken" and people are "basically pouring out to you things that they wouldn't be able to tell someone else." Along this journey, Ms. Jackie and her team tries to show—rather than tell—families how to navigate these bureaucracies. "We are by their side navigating these institutions. Going in there with them." Again, Ms. Jackie brings it back to "what my elders did for me" when they brought her to the table and led by example.

As I have written about elsewhere, a *pedagogy of commitment* provides stability and consistency that families can depend on (Watson 2012). Ms. Jackie echoes this point: "When I'm out here in the community or they walk in here, they say, '*You're still here!*'" She elaborates, "I think that one of the things that a lot of the young people I have crossed paths with will tell me is, '*The only thing I can feel good about Ms. Jackie is that you are still here and you are constant.*'" Ms. Jackie leans forward and looks down at her folded hands resting on the table between us. She begins to shake her head as she looks up and talks about the "abandonment issues that a lot of our young people and families go through." That is why it is imperative to have "consistency" and "somebody that they can always go to." She repeats, "It's *very, very* important."

Unfortunately, Ms. Jackie laments, "We don't have a lot of those consistent people that stay around for decades that are going to be there for the people that are the most vulnerable." Perhaps some people burn out or relocate, or a new reform emerges, or funding streams change course: whatever the reason, there is a lot of transience. For families who are surviving through various instabilities, impermanence can be devastating. It makes sense, then, that an important component of Ms. Jackie's effectiveness is her lifelong commitment to Black children and families in Sacramento. For Ms. Jackie, the seed of social change is the development of reliable, respectful, revolutionary relationships.

She grins with joy as she says, "We were just at the baby shower this weekend." Ms. Jackie refers to the intergenerational impact that occurs by doing the same kind of work, over time, in the same location. Place matters. "Most of those mothers" at the baby shower used to be "a lot of my young people." Ms. Jackie was able to "touch their lives," and they are still a part of her extended family. She laughs under her breath: "They were swarming us like bees on Saturday!" During this celebration, Ms. Jackie was consistent with her mentoring and counseled the new mom on the "importance of loving this baby like I love them."

Engage My People

"You have to love what you do. You have to love the people you serve," exclaims Ms. Jackie, who is skeptical that love is a trainable attribute. As with authenticity, it needs to be integral to a person's walk in the world. Quite frankly, the only people who fully and completely know about the Black experience are Black people. But she is realistic that it takes all kinds of people to improve a community. Ms. Jackie's pragmatism comes forward just as she leans toward me: "All those kind of things to really be authentic in the delivery of anything" from meetings with child care to meals that show you genuinely care and see the fullness of someone. I nod and agree, "It's holistic and wholesome." "Exactly," and Ms. Jackie continues. The "underserved population has already gone through enough! And they don't need someone that is gonna take them through more!"

Unlike some service providers, Ms. Jackie explains, "We're not just giving them a bus pass and leave them. If you need a bus pass, there is some other stuff going on. We need to sit down and really open up a case and open up this Pandora's box and figure out what else is going on." Ms. Jackie and her staff provide hands-on wraparound care and intensive case management with the goal of families becoming "stable enough to stand on their own." The work is not easy, and it is more than full time. The current caseload of RFCE is "about 44 and growing."

After three decades of serving Black families, Ms. Jackie seems like an expert. Hearing this observation, she chuckles a bit and describes what she was like when she first started working in the projects back when it was called Franklin Villa. By day it looked calm and quiet, but by nighttime it was like "New Jack City." During this time, Ms. Jackie was working for a housing corporation: "I was the only African American at the time that worked in this department . . . *Of course, they're gonna send the Black girl to Jean Parkway.*"

"Now I'm Black," Ms. Jackie states, and "most of the community was Black." But she later realized, "I didn't know anything!" She shakes her head and folds her arms: the families would not engage with her *at all*. Ms. Jackie doesn't like to fail and wanted to be an advocate, but she did not know how to build the trust necessary to get the work done. "I went home and I prayed on it. . . . I'm not giving up on this one. There [has] got to be a way to engage my people." She started anew and left the adults alone. "I'm going to start with the kids," she decided. Ms. Jackie started a "little afterschool program" in "one of the four-plex units," and ten kids showed up. After some time passed and the program started to grow, she asked the children, "Why do your parents not want to talk with me?" The babies were clear as day and told her bluntly: "They think you're the police."

Again, Ms. Jackie had to reevaluate her strategy: "I had system written on my face. . . . I was going out there in my little suits and my heels, and all of this stuff." To gain the trust of the neighborhood, she literally gave herself a makeover and toned it all down. "I went and got me some colors" and "some jeans." Essentially, she humbled herself to the tone of the community, and families started to talk to her. "And they would tell me, *We thought you were Po Po. We didn't know you were here to help us.*" Slowly a partnership began to be forged from everyone's love for the children. "The gang bangers would send their kids over" and would share with Ms. Jackie that "even though I'm out here in the streets, I want my kids to get an education"; in exchange for this support, "we'll protect the place where you provide the afterschool program." She explains that they literally had "this handshake deal" that anywhere the "kids did activities was off-limits." From that point on, the center began to thrive. Over the years, she worked with nearly one hundred kids, and they defied the stereotypes ("bottom of the barrel not doing anything successful") and are now college educated. She is especially proud that many of them went "off to college and came back to the community. My dream for them is to always come back and serve. . . . Because who knows your community better than you?" Ms. Jackie repeats, "I need you to come back and serve."

Collective Action

After decades of working with the housing authority, Ms. Jackie had her eyes on retirement. "I had done my thirty years, I was ready to retire," she says with a smirk. "It was time to go and then" something unexpected happened: "I was sitting in Phoenix Park" and felt something stir deep inside that said, "You are not finished."

"So I started my own 501(c)(3)," which is now the thriving Rose Family Creative Empowerment Center. She has been steadily expanding the service model over the last six years, with a tremendous amount of support from the Sierra Health Foundation and BCLC. She explains that BCLC has connected her to systems change and neighborhood networks in a whole new way: it provided Ms. Jackie and her colleagues the opportunity to join forces across the region and strategically advocate for the needs of the African American community, alongside its members. She asserts that the system needed to be held accountable, and BCLC became a tool to "vet these folks" who are mandated to improve the quality of life for poor folks and who are disproportionately African American. She cites Child Protective Services (CPS) as an example: its staff often "hold families' feet to the fire" with deliverables so that they can keep or regain custody of their children. With the help of BCLC, Ms. Jackie and others created checkpoints to monitor CPS staff's cultural competencies and are using *cultural brokers* to foster bridges between families and social workers. Now when a case is referred to CPS, its staff are culturally sensitive. "Parents are being accountable to certain deliverables," says Ms. Jackie, but her job is to also hold the system's "feet to the fire." In other words, deliverables should not be one-directional; they need to be reciprocal.

Over the years, BCLC has helped develop a vital partnership between community members and social services. Relationships have improved. She explains, "The Black Child Legacy Campaign has given us the latitude to actually present and produce this kind of model where we are "working *with* CPS, working *with* DHA, working *with* Probation, working *with* the police department, working *with* SETA (Sacramento Employment & Training Administration)" so that Black children in this city survive and thrive.

Dynamic social services and innovative institutional practices are fundamental to equity, and yet these systems alone cannot solve every problem. Even at the grassroots level, critical reflection is needed for healthy development and growth. Ms. Jackie brings up a space for intentional improvements. She reflects, once again, on the powerful village that raised her and surmises, "I had that balance." I ask what she means. Ms. Jackie worries that there is an unevenness right now and that it takes both male and female leadership to nourish a thriving neighborhood. She is forthright in her critiques: "There is not that balance anymore in our communities. It's pretty much female-dominated. And females are always in these males' ears trying to tell them what to do." Ms. Jackie yearns for harmonious, collective accountability—and it starts with how we reflect on our own identities while simultaneously elevating one another. She is straight to the point: "So anytime I get a chance at bringing a male and raising up these young males to become the leaders of these young men it's *very, very* important for me to do that" because "I can't teach manhood."

Black Childhood Is Precious

We started our conversation with the past, and here we are, again, looking backward. Ms. Jackie's earliest memory of racism stems from elementary school when she was in the second grade. The school she attended was predominantly white, and she was "always singled out" with "racial slurs." Her expression is stoic and unbothered as she tells me, "They would basically use the n-word quite often." These experiences inside school were drastically different from those in the community that raised her. In a soft tone that soothes the soul, she utters slowly, "Black childhood is precious."

"It's always at the top of my agenda" to ensure that "Black children know their greatness through the past, but for others to know our greatness too because people can't see the greatness in you unless they know your history." Without a knowledge of African civilizations and ongoing legacies of liberation, she says, "How are we gonna feel great? How are we gonna resonate in that greatness if we don't know it? And oftentimes our kids don't know it. They absolutely don't know."

The Black Child Legacy Campaign presents a bolder horizon for the city of Sacramento. On this horizon, BCLC is rising with people like Ms. Jackie Rose who are holding Black children at the center—like the sun. These children's lives are the peak of a city's quest for progress, a community's need for partnerships, and a people's continued perseverance.

Black people build worlds within worlds. They always have. These alternative spaces exemplify life and liberation, joy and justice. The struggle for Black excellence and equity is real and can be cruel, yet there is beauty in the fight. There is profound purpose in Black power. In our final moments together, I provide Ms. Jackie with some prompts. Her answers pour out poetically like a future calling itself forward:

> Black power . . . *feels free.*
> Freedom to me . . . *sounds like a Marvin Gaye song.*
> When I look into our past . . . *I see nothing but greatness.*
> When I look in the mirror . . . *I see nothing but beauty.*
> When I look into our future . . . *I see hope.*
> I am fighting against . . . *a system that doesn't include us.*
> I'm fighting to . . . *dismantle the system.*
> I'm building . . . *a legacy of leaders who will carry out my vision.*
> I love . . . *what I do.*

Part 5
LESSONS

This concluding part, "Lessons," raises the question: What can I learn from the Black Child Legacy Campaign? What began as a plan to reduce Black infant mortality by focusing on seven neighborhoods with five strategies evolved into a network of community organizations, families, leaders, and government entities collaborating and "creating sustainable strategies and building on each neighborhood's amazing strengths, qualities, and unique attributes." If you are a mayor, educator, youth advocate, student, parent, nonprofit leader, or community leader, this section should be of great interest. Heather Gonzalez, Amaya Noguera-Mujica, Adiyah Ma'at Obolu, Torry Winn, and Vajra Watson discuss their experiences and offer lessons, insights, and recommendations. This part provides perspectives from mental health advocates, social services leaders, educational researchers, and student-artist-activists. It concludes with *futures matter* with chapter 22, "Reopening: Future Forward."

THERE'S STILL MORE TO DO
Community Reflection

Heather Gonzalez

In a moment where cries heard across the globe have united people to stand against systemic racism and the continual perpetuation of institutional harm and violence against BIPOC folks, the Black Child Legacy Campaign has never been timelier. BCLC remains affirmed as "just" and essential to reducing the insidious racial harm woven into our system's very fabric. Much like the nation, Sacramento has a long history of "turning its head" from the preventable, perpetual, and continual disproportionate death rates afflicting our African American babies and youth in the four focus areas that BCLC has aimed to mitigate.

At its conception, BCLC's mission was lofty yet imperative. We set out to reduce the named disparities of mortality by 20 percent in a five-year timeframe in the four areas of highest impact across Sacramento County: perinatal conditions, unsafe sleep-related outcomes, child abuse and neglect, and third-party homicide. Each of the seven Community Incubator Leads were strategically placed and given the charge to build with and follow the direction of neighborhood leaders, residents, and stakeholders. Together, they were mandated to develop neighborhood-specific strategies to reduce these preventable outcomes while creating sustainable strategies and alliances to continue building on each neighborhood's amazing strengths, qualities, and unique attributes.

Having spent my entire career serving the greater Sacramento area within the nonprofit field, I soon noticed something beautiful and striking that set BCLC apart from other agencies and programs: the documented reduction of mortality rates was one of the main indicators of success. BCLC did not rely on widgets or predetermined program outcomes developed by folks far removed from and unaffected by the conditions being addressed. Furthermore, there was an intentional approach to ensure that strategies were developed by BIPOC folks from many walks of life, were led by BIPOC folks in and from the most affected neighborhoods, and were unapologetically designed to serve BIPOC folks through every service and support; this commitment demonstrated that approaching service through *targeted universalism*, steeped in values of racial equity that were consistently upheld throughout all functions of the work, is not only possible but is also an essential component to getting to the root of the issues and moving the needle forward. To be clear, racism and systemic racism are the root causes of Sacramento's long history of preventable and disproportionate mortality rates for our African American families. BCLC remained rooted in that understanding and has been successful in its mission because it never watered down the narrative or wavered from that truth in seeking funding and support from those unaffected by these ills.

To be neutral in the face of racism is not enough. One must be unapologetically antiracist in action and commit to a lifetime of service, self-work, and reflection to deconstruct our own internalized and implicit attachment to racist ideologies while simultaneously dismantling social constructs and systemic laws, policies, practices, and procedures that perpetuate racist outcomes that continuously harm communities of color. White folks in Sacramento have, historically and continuously, led nonprofit initiatives and organizations funded to serve BIPOC communities and have built their careers on the backs of the communities they have been tasked to "serve" while never being held accountable or holding themselves accountable for closing the gaps of health, wealth, and meaningful representation within leadership and voice in spaces of impact. By design, BCLC demonstrates that this antiquated and harmful approach can be changed through a commitment to racial equity principles, action, and an abundance of accountability.

The work is not easy, but it is sacred, it is urgent, and it is imperative that we get it right. We have had our wins and are so proud of our success in accomplishing our goals of reducing mortality disparities in some of the focus areas. However, this is only the beginning. More resources are needed: more bodies, more support. The reality of this work is that African American babies and youth are dying. Collectively we are not doing enough about it in Sacramento County. Some of the stories make the news, and you will see fair weather providers vying for the spotlight to get accolades in the moment, public officials making empty promises for the news outlets, and folks pontificating on the needs. Folks will be outraged for a few weeks and then move on to the next issue, while our families, with little support, are left to put together the shattered pieces that remain.

Most affected families are supported and held by the folks serving on the frontline, who have little resources to provide; those who tirelessly show up to serve—who move from scene to scene and from family to family, and who facilitate as much healing and support as able to ease the impacts families experience after losing their child(ren)—have even less resources for themselves. The emotional labor, crushing weight, and vicarious trauma are real for most of those who show up in service for the cause. It is heartbreaking for me to admit that I cannot remember the number of families we have supported who lost a child for preventable reasons, and that thought plays over and over in my mind. It haunts me in quiet moments. Each life is sacred. The fact that there have been too many children lost to remember each one is gut wrenching, but real. Nonetheless, we carry the pain and their families' cries in our hearts and souls, and righteous rage rolls out of our mouths when we speak on these issues and call for change in honor of those unable to be present in the arenas where we battle.

Of all the important causes to fight for, I cannot think of ones more important than those of the Black Child Legacy Campaign. This work is essential, urgent, and sacred, and we are centuries late in addressing it. I am forever grateful and humbled to have been allowed into these sacred spaces and to serve alongside so many impactful healers, leaders, activists, advocates, change agents, public servants, and social justice warriors. It has been an honor to serve our beautiful community, to be trusted to support families in their darkest of times, and to walk alongside them as they find a way to carry on.

19

WELLNESS WORKS

Community Reflection

Amaya Noguera-Mujica

The Community Responsive Wellness Program for the African American/Black communities of Sacramento (previously known as the Trauma Informed Wellness Program) was launched in 2021 from the work and efforts of the Black Child Legacy Campaign. For BCLC to achieve its mission of reducing Black deaths in the Sacramento area, there grew the recognition of the need for mental health services specifically designed to address the needs of Black communities.

Since its creation in 2015, BCLC has made visible the numerous factors that contribute to the mental health crises in the Black community and has played a leading role in devising a layered response to the oppressive dynamics that directly affect the health and well-being of Black people of all backgrounds. As a result of these efforts, a nuanced and responsive approach to addressing historic barriers to mental health care emerged. Today, a mental health delivery system is providing services to Sacramento's Black community from multiple entry points.

In the wake of the police killing of Stephon Clark in 2018, the Sacramento County Division of Behavioral Health Services and local stakeholders formed the Cultural Competence Committee Ad Hoc Workgroup. This workgroup was charged with designing community listening sessions to give African American/ Black community members an opportunity to reflect on how trauma has affected their community and to express their needs and desires for a more responsive social welfare system. As a result of these sessions, the community developed a recommendation for a new prevention and early intervention program that would address the mental health and wellness needs of the African American/

Black community. From the outset, this initiative was inclusive of lesbian, gay, bisexual, transgender, and queer community members who also experienced or were exposed to high rates of trauma.

BCLC's profound impact is now widely recognized and unquestionable. Throughout the Black community of Sacramento, there is widespread praise and acclaim for its services. However, there are still great challenges: the residual effects of generations of oppressive conditions, collective trauma, and pain are still quite acute and prevalent. Collectively, we draw inspiration and insight from Joy DeGruy:

> We can experience this injury (trauma) physically, emotionally, psychologically, and/or spiritually. Traumas can upset our equilibrium and well-being. If a trauma is severe enough, it can distort our attitudes and beliefs. Such distortions often result in dysfunctional behaviors, and unwanted consequences, this pattern is magnified exponentially when a person repeatedly experiences severe trauma, and it is much worse when the traumas are caused by human beings. (2005, 8)

In November 2020, the Sacramento County Board of Supervisors declared racism a public health crisis. Their acknowledgment, although helpful in that it recognized the source of the mental health crisis, came too late. Over the years there have been too many casualties of police and neighborhood violence to count. Racism in its institutional, structural, and interpersonal forms has been a threat to the mental health of Black people for many years. For this reason, when we talk about mental health in the Community Responsive Wellness Program, we acknowledge how conditions such as poverty, unemployment, housing, and food security, as well as inadequate education, contribute to prevalent mental health problems. We recognize that these conditions undermine the mental health and well-being of many Black people and place large numbers of children at risk of future trauma.

In cities throughout the United States, it is evident that it is not safe for Black people to not be treated for mental illness. In too many cases, Black people with untreated mental illnesses are perceived and treated as a criminal threat. Many of the residents we work with have witnessed the firsthand effects of navigating racist, unresponsive mental health systems and the dangers of being forced to rely on law enforcement to address mental health needs. Police officers and institutions that are ostensibly designed to help, such as social service agencies, are frequently unable to provide the mental health support that people direly need. For this reason, it is so important that we respond to the mental health crisis collectively and with a sense of urgency.

The work of the Community Responsive Wellness Program is just beginning. In coming years, we aim to improve mental health services in the Sacramento area by fulfilling our vision and mission.

Community Responsive Wellness Program's Vision and Mission

We envision a revitalized and healthy Black community in Sacramento. We believe this is possible through an increased sense of agency, connectedness, and awareness of health and wellness needs, greater participation in support services, and trusting relationships with mental health service providers (MHSPs). We envision MHSPs who actively seek to understand the context for the prevalent mental health needs in Sacramento's Black community, develop programming and services that respond to those needs, and provide intervention and preventive support to Black individuals and families.

To realize this vision, we commit to the following four actions:

1. educating the public on common mental health needs and wellness practices for Black people in Sacramento
2. supporting access to culturally responsive mental health services
3. building the capacity of mental health service providers to identify and be responsive to commonly occurring mental health needs within the Black community
4. ensuring that service providers maintain an accurate account of the context of mental health needs in Sacramento's Black communities

Realizing our mission and vision will take time and work. In the short term, our primary goals are to normalize conversations regarding mental health, thereby reducing the stigma many attach to receiving mental health support. By doing so, we believe that we can collectively work toward healing.

One of the most successful groups to come out of BCLC is Healing the Hood and the work of its crisis response team. This team serves to support individuals and families in crisis, and its members make themselves available around the clock to respond to crises in the community. Many team members have experienced trauma themselves. Their insights and understanding make it possible for them to support others in need and thereby help bring about a reduction in Black child deaths. Although the work performed by this team has been phenomenal, it has also become clear that its members are also in need of mental health support. They have become first responders, and if they are to continue to serve in this capacity, they will need help.

Because of BCLC's work we can better understand where gaps in services are present. This has made it possible to steadily provide more strategic support to our community partners and the larger communities that we serve. The good news is that BCLC's efforts have contributed to a reduction in Black child deaths. However, there is more work to be done. The harmful effects of police-sanctioned violence witnessed worldwide, with little to no consequence, continue to traumatize the Black community. Additionally, the heavy economic strains and health burdens created by the COVID-19 pandemic and the ongoing effects of intergenerational poverty have left many Black communities in dire need of mental health services and prevention programs that can provide healing and care on a large scale.

Although there is much work that needs to be done to improve Black mental health in this country, BCLC is showing that we can take decisive action to make tangible improvements. The newly created Community Responsive Wellness Program is a prime example of the ongoing work that is needed to strengthen mental health support in Black communities. We must ensure that all members of the Black community can turn their attention from merely surviving to promoting a holistic approach to wellness. To address the needs of adolescents who are in the midst of a major mental health crisis, senior citizens who are too often suffering from prolonged isolation, and many others who are stressed out by racism and economic uncertainty, we have to continue to rely on our creativity, dedication, and understanding of the complexities of our oppression to create and design programs that both prevent negative outcomes and increase the likelihood of positive outcomes. If we want to see flourishing in our communities, we must do this work on a larger scale.

The goal of the Community Responsive Wellness Program is to create opportunities for Black people to heal. We do this while acknowledging that we are an extremely diverse people, encompassing all our intersectional identities. We found that it is imperative to include those from the LGBTQ community, recent immigrants and refugees, and others who are frequently marginalized and silenced despite their needs. The complexities of how Black bodies are seen, felt, and received in this country make it difficult to design solutions and prevention programs, but that does not mean we cannot try our best. We can learn from successful community-oriented projects such as the Black Child Legacy Campaign to develop new programs that can respond to the needs of the most deeply impacted and vulnerable members of our communities.

REFERENCE

DeGruy, Joy. 2005. *Post Traumatic Slave Syndrome: America's Legacy of Enduring Injury and Healing.* Portland, OR: Joy DeGruy Publications.

THE FIRE THIS TIME

Youth Reflection

Adiyah Ma'at Obolu

My name is Adiyah Obolu, and I am a high school junior in the Sacramento area. Poetry has become an outlet for me to express myself and process the atrocities of the world. Since I was a toddler, I have been attending poetry slams and, even then, I was astonished by how much I could learn about recollection and history from a form of art. As I got older, I began to create my own poetry to honor my story and the future I want to create for the world. Now, I am a poet in Sacramento Area Youth Speaks (SAYS), performing on national stages to engage, inspire, and educate my listeners.

My poem, "Forest Fire," is inspired by the astonishing Sonia Sanchez poem, "Catch the Fire," featured in the "Opening" of this book. In the poem, Sanchez calls on us to look toward the fire of Blackness. Blackness that is resilient and powerful, revolutionary and beautiful, passionate and purposeful. Sanchez pushes us to find the fire that is already kindled inside us to make change and reach our full potential. Spread the fire through community, through our schools, through love—and once we set the fire in ourselves, it has the inherent potential to spread across generations. Even with the day-to-day hardships of being Black, Sanchez reminds us that we have a fire that can never be extinguished: no matter how small the flame is, our fire is always being kindled.

In my poem, I try to find that fire inside myself. I wrote it at a time when I felt a loss of hope for the world. After witnessing the mass uprisings of 2020, I was eager to see a country geared more toward racial justice. But as the protests and news coverage began to die down, I felt a loss of momentum. How could so much happen in a couple of months, and all there is to show is a Black Lives

Matter painting at the White House? Or corporations using Black lives to make sales even when they are exploiting Black workers in the process? What hope was there when the only thing this country had to give us was performative activism?

With these feelings looming, some of the only ways I can cope is to write poetry. So I wrote. I honored my fire as I sought to kindle it a little more. I pondered where my drive to make change was, where my endless dreams of revolution were. I sought to reconnect with my fire and allow it to spread, faster than ever known.

My poem questions the status quo and what true justice looks like. But, let us never forget our morals when using this powerful fire. Let us not get so lost in a task or a project that we forget what we are doing it for. Let us use this fire to create roots and branch out trees but not burn the forest down. This fire comes with the inherent responsibility to spread and nurture it, but not burn our history away or lose the knowledge of our ancestors. Our fire spreads light, our fire decolonizes our minds, our fire dreams drastically and unapologetically.

In addition to writing poetry, I also seek to imagine the future and to make it. I started my own podcast, *Our Justice Journey*, which is a series of conversations with social justice warriors giving advice to youth on how to make change. I worked cooperatively with my school's Black Student Union to create a district-wide Student Bill of Rights that is currently in process before it is finally implemented as policy in our district. Throughout all this, I have learned what justice work needs, and what it takes is fire. The fire to keep going, the fire that lights the way, the fire that spreads and inspires.

I often return to this poem when I feel I have lost my momentum to create change, not only to learn about the world but also to create and imagine sustainable solutions for change. I use my fire to change policy, to inspire, to create projects that push my community to our full potential. Being Black in Sacramento is simultaneously beautiful and painful. The beauty of Blackness that can surround you in certain areas is comforting and feels like home. But knowing that those very spaces are targets is traumatic. When Stephon Clark was killed in his grandmother's backyard, you realize that you are not safe even in your home. Even with SacPD being run by a Black man and one of the officers who killed Clark being a Black policeman. When white supremacists could come to your school, as they did to mine in September 2021, and target the Black Student Union with an issue that has nothing to do with them, you realize you are not safe even in your school. But even with these hardships, the beauty of Blackness is incomparable.

I am inspired by all the powerful Black solutionaries here in Sacramento. I think about the Black youth who show up eagerly when I intern with *Foreign*

Native to host youth pop-up shops and learn entrepreneurship skills. Or my peers whom I work with in a nonprofit called *Youth Voices Sacramento*, which seeks to put youth first. My amazing co-hosts on the podcast *Black vs. the Board of Education* who call out the education system and embody the change we need to see in our districts. And my peers whom I work with on *College to Career Ready* (CCR) to create equitable schooling and better opportunities for Black youth across the region. Blackness is beautiful, and it is also resilient. Hope continues to multiply, even with new barriers. Black youth inspire me to make change; I know our future will be filled with even more fire.

"Catch the Fire" and "Forest Fire" push us to honor the fire of Blackness, of justice, of global love. Together we have the capability to drastically improve the world. As SAYS director and poet Patrice Hill teaches us, "Every Black child deserves to have a legacy." Every Black child is our ancestors' living, breathing legacy. And as Ta-Nehsi Coates echoes, "They made us into a race. We made ourselves into a people." We are the remembrance. We are the recollection. We are the becoming of the legacy of an unstoppable fire that has been kindled since the beginning of time. We are forest fire.

"Forest Fire"
Where is my fire?
I want it to catch and then inspire
Where is my fire?
Lost hope but with that how do we cope
Where is my fire?
Is it hiding inside me and I have yet to ignite it?
Where is my fire?
Cause it was just us against the world
Most haven't even touched their motherlands soil
I often toil with the world
With our progression and oppression
I toil if integration was really ever the way
How do I right now make change?
And emancipate myself from mental slavery
But for some it's all they've ever known
As we cast a vote for hope
But how do I imagine horizons worth climbing for?
Or money worth buyin for?
Do we really think the revolution is worth dyin for?
I'm sick of these denying sources
white supremacist courses

On some don't bring up the corpses
America is living on borrowed time
Never indicted for their crimes
As we climb the very tree they hung Black folks off of
And then gaslight the Black communities' intergenerational trauma
Would they know what to do?
Martin, Malcom, would they know how to fight for truth?
Selassie, Assata, would they know how to uplift the youth?
But it's our turn to find a new tree and tend the soil
Branch off roots and inspire
Keep our eye on the goal, global love is what we seek to acquire
We ain't the fire next time, we the fire right now
But can we use it for justice and not burn the whole forest down

—Adiyah Obolu

TRANSFORMATIVE JUSTICE COMMUNITY

Insights and Implications

Lawrence "Torry" Winn and Vajra M. Watson

The Black Child Legacy Campaign's plan to reduce deaths of African American children in Sacramento County is a community-driven movement supported by a multilayered support system. Since 2015, the strategic plan developed by the Steering Committee on the Reduction of African American Child Deaths (SC-RAACD), "African American Children Matter: What We Must Do Now," has focused on seven neighborhoods and five strategies to transform public systems and increase community engagement with and by local families and communities. The five strategies guiding the path to reduce Black child deaths are as follows:

1. *Develop communications and information systems* through a dual approach to messaging that engages the broader community in BCLC work while expanding reach within seven targeted neighborhoods
2. *Promote advocacy and policy transformation* through a push for local and statewide policy advocacy and initiatives to create systemic change
3. *Promote equitable investment and systemic impact* through focusing on systemic approaches to programming
4. *Provide coordinated systems of support* reflecting a systemic approach to wraparound intervention and prevention services that positions a trusted community-based organization as a hub for cross-agency collaboration

5. *Assess data-driven accountability and collective impact* through a quality assessment process that includes eleven quality dimensions and measures progress toward the BCLC's goals of reducing the four leading causes of Black children's deaths

Between 2015 and 2020, the impact and successes of the five strategies were well documented by BCLC and in the media. The March 2020 annual report, *Black Child Legacy Campaign: An Action Guide for Engaging and Strengthening the Social Safety Net*, highlights the following accomplishments:

- In 2016, BCLC surpassed the 10 percent goal of reducing child mortality after only one year of implementation.
- In 2018, after just three years of implementation, BCLC
  ○ reduced the rate of African American child deaths by 25 percent
  ○ reduced the rate of African American infant deaths by 23 percent
  ○ reduced the disparity in infant sleep-related deaths by more than 50 percent
  ○ saw zero juvenile homicides in 2018 and 2019
  ○ assigned nearly 200 cultural broker referrals through the Sacramento County Cultural Broker Program
- On March 2, 2019, the success of the Black Child Legacy Campaign was recognized by the National Association of Counties Health Steering Committee.

Although these data points describe the targeted outcomes, the collected and analyzed quantitative data only tell part of BCLC's story about reducing African American child deaths. They do not provide insight into the challenges, promises, experiences, learnings, and personal stories that shed light on the effectiveness of the five strategies. To gain a deeper understanding of BCLC, we posed questions in a qualitative evaluation, such as the following:

- What did the participants experience?
- How is this connected to the participant's personal story and what connects them to BCLC?
- What worked, and what did not work and why?
- How is anti-Blackness or race a factor?
- What do community leaders deem successful?
- How do they envision the future?
- Do they believe this work is sustainable?

Many of the questions were guided by the five pedagogical stances of engaging transformative justice: *History Matters, Race Matters, Justice Matters, Language Matters,* and *Futures Matter* (Winn 2018, 2019). The findings drawn from interviews, archival data, and participant observations provide insights for similar communities considering implementing frameworks to improve the life chances of Black families and youth.

An Empowering Name: Leaving a Legacy for Black Children

> It's always at the top of my agenda to ensure Black children know their greatness through the past, but for others to know our greatness, too, because people can't see the greatness in you unless they know your history.
>
> —Community Incubator Lead staff member

BCLC's communications and information systems strategy is best explained by the name given to the initiative, the Black Child Legacy Campaign. Educational researcher Maisha T. Winn (2018) has shown that *language matters* because words or images may either uplift or deflate the morale of those associated with a particular group. Recognizing the need for an inspirational and forward-looking name for implementation, SC-RAACD led a community-engaged process that yielded the name "Black Child Legacy Campaign." BCLC has become known as a positive and inspiring movement all over the Sacramento Valley and is motivating individuals and agencies to work collectively to improve the quality of life for African Americans. When asked about the effectiveness of BCLC's messaging and its ability to share information with the community and families, many BCLC participants mentioned the purposeful naming of the effort. For example, one BCLC participant stated, "Legacy is the antithesis of death." The name of the movement is asset-based and challenges mainstream deficit models steeped in anti-Blackness and antiracism (Kendi 2019). Rather than leading conversations about Black child deaths with naming conventions and verbal framing that signal hopelessness, despair, and a lack of agency, the strategic and purposeful use of "legacy" emphasizes a fruitful past and bright future—despite the persistent systemic barriers that hinder the progress of African American families. Several participants commented about the significance of BCLC's name:

> "I knew very little of the Black Child Legacy Campaign prior to and at the time of, the name really had no significance to me because I heard

the title Black put on a lot of different organizations, yet . . . I was more so optimistic."

"Black Child Legacy, you want to speak a message of hope."

"I'm building a legacy of leaders."

By removing the stigma associated with Sacramento County services, the name and mission of the BCLC have made it easier for partner agencies to do outreach and offer services to community residents in the seven neighborhoods. According to one BCLC member, "BCLC gives me cover as a county worker to provide assistance in ways I could not because of the stigma that comes with working for the county."

The Sierra Health Foundation was responsible for ensuring the success of the brand through its implementation of the communications strategy. BCLC has been publicized in multiple ways, including in widely distributed brochures, event displays, media coverage, and "swag" apparel. For example, at meetings of the Sacramento County Board of Supervisors and the City Council and local events such as Dr. Martin Luther King Jr. celebrations and marches, Sacramento Kings games, health fairs, and community town halls, BCLC's green-and-black logo can be found on scarves, posters, t-shirts, handouts, and banners. At the January 29, 2019, meeting of the Sacramento County Board of Supervisors, more than one hundred BCLC supporters either wore BCLC t-shirts or had brochures in their hands. BCLC's logo and collateral material are displayed at every one of its events. For example, in the North Highlands-Foothill Farms and Oak Park CIL offices, literature and informative resources are neatly displayed throughout the lobbies and workspaces. Posters of Black families hang on the walls, and one-page resource lists are readily accessible for guests.

The BCLC website, annual reports, and media releases/write ups provide another means of communication and branding to get key messaging out to the community. The website features images of Black families (mothers and sons, fathers and daughters, and so on) and Black people celebrating together or volunteering. The interactive digital platform provides information, data for all seven neighborhoods, videos, links to past interviews, upcoming events, and PDFs of every published report. BCLC has been featured in the *Sacramento Bee*, *Sacramento Observer*, and local television news programs. In July 2019, Priska Neely, a Los Angeles public radio station reporter, described lessons from BCLC that should be applied by Los Angeles to achieve similarly positive results. Other reporters wrote articles about the succes of BCLC between 2017 and 2020.[1]

Insights Related to Communicating and Connecting

1. *Language Matters.* The name "Black Child Legacy Campaign" is a powerful and inspired public call for action. The name and the promotion of BCLC challenge deficit paradigms steeped in anti-Blackness.
2. *Promotion/swag is key to messaging.* Promotion of BCLC at public events and forums encouraged urgent awareness of the issues facing the African American community. Swag gear/materials such as scarves, posters, and t-shirts help promote BCLC, resulting in more awareness and significant cultural shifts.
3. *Relationships build bridges.* BCLC's intimate connection with local communities affected by child deaths and its relationships with county agencies are making it easier for social services and community leaders to work together.

Social and Political Capital: Access to Opportunities and Resources

> We all receive training for this work. Now I have more opportunities.
>
> —Crisis intervention worker

The advocacy and policy transformation strategy has been implemented primarily through a Community Leadership Roundtable comprising residents who volunteer in the seven neighborhoods. Roundtable members meet monthly and receive training in advocacy, crisis response, and evaluation of the quality of CIL implementation. This process provides a platform to foster unity and address issues with one voice. Representatives of CILs, the seven community-based organizations that lead BCLC at the neighborhood level, have presented at City Council and county meetings, board commissions, and policy-making forums. CILs have been able to cultivate relationships with local police officers, elected officials, universities, and businesses—coordinating efforts to maximize impact.

Youth projects such as Youth Participatory Action Research, SAYS spoken word events such as Poetic Service Announcements, and the Kings and Queens Rise Youth Basketball League promote advocacy for youth programs and reduction of violence. One CIL staff member states that we have these programs so the youth can "use their voices, provide solutions, discuss their fears, and actively collaborate for brighter futures."

Insights Related to Promoting Advocacy and Policy

1. *Folk love to learn and build.* Trainings provide opportunities for community members to network with one another, leading to an exchange of ideas, trust, and support.
2. *Common goals are essential.* The coordination and collaboration of the CILs around common goals and outcomes is key to changing policy at the local and state level.
3. *Advocacy and policy transformation must be intergenerational.*

A Countywide Infrastructure to Support Black Children

> Seeing that services can collaborate, we don't have to be in our silos; we're able to each align ourselves with what best supports we can give them and then once we feel like they've completed that job, employment, mental health services, then we kind of reevaluate where they're at.
>
> —CIL staff member

The equitable investment and systematic impact strategy was originally envisioned for implementation through an Interagency Children's Policy Council comprising executive leadership, elected officials, and other policy makers from county agencies that affect the lives of low-income and vulnerable children and families. Although it was subsequently decided not to create the Interagency Children's Policy Council, there are many instances of coordination across public agencies. The most significant examples are the out-stationing of county staff in neighborhood-led organizations and the use of multidisciplinary teams made up of county and community service providers to provide wraparound services to families and children.

Before BCLC was created, there was limited collaboration between nonprofit organizations and government agencies, nor were there common goals and a shared vision. Nonprofits and county agencies often worked and operated in silos within their communities. By placing staff in the offices of community-based organizations, county agencies have built relationships with and through local resources and residents. Staff placed in CILs represent Child Protective Services, Department of Human Assistance, Probation Department, and the Sacramento Employment & Training Administration. The significance of the multidisciplinary teams is best described by the service providers who participated in them:

"Through Black Child Legacy Campaign, we're able to go above and beyond and dive deeper and be intentional on the cultural matches, be intentional on the wraparound services and all of that other great stuff that is important to actually bridging the gap."—CIL staff member

"First time as a county worker getting the chance to sit next to and across from others doing similar work. I see these people on TV or read about them. Now we are doing this together."—multidisciplinary team (MDT) staff member

"I've been with the county for eighteen years and I've been outstationed ten years. So, this is the first time that I've actually been able to see the people whose name I recognize on email or whose name I see."—MTD staff member

As discussed in chapter 3, "History Matters: Realities of Redlining in Sacramento," communities that have a higher percentage of African Americans have experienced disinvestment and faced economic challenges since the 1960s. The partnership between BCLC and Sacramento County provides CILs with human capital, making it possible for them to deliver the services and resources needed by the most vulnerable and under-resourced.

Challenges remain despite this equitable approach. One emerging challenge concerns the sustainability of the funding needed to continue making progress and improving the lives of Black families. "What happens if the county changes course or [County Supervisor] Serna is no longer around?" one MDT staff member wondered. She added, "Sustainability depends on the county's support." Other concerns include the high turnover rate among CILs. "The reason for turnover in the CILs is better pay. They are talented and inspiring but need to be compensated more," commented an MDT staff member. Between 2017 and 2020, only a few CILs retained one or two leaders for multiple years, and most experienced an exodus of three to five staff members only after six to twelve months on the job. Short-lived tenure makes consistent record keeping, data collection, and community outreach more difficult and reduces institutional knowledge. Some of these challenges have been offset by support from CILs with lower staff turnover and a strong network of community partners.

Insights Related to Equitable Investment and Systematic Impact

1. *BCLC has leveraged its collaboration of seven communities and multiple partners to procure more funds.* Increased social and political

coordination and access to resources and opportunities are key to systematic change.

2. *Staff turnover has been offset by strong relationships with community partners and support from other CILs.*

3. *Systematic impact is only as effective as the investment in the sustainability of the strategies.* Doubts about the continuation of funding lessen the morale of participants.

Local and Countywide Social Network of Change Agents

> Building partnerships is difficult. It means you have to let go of something, but you also have to invite others in. Ultimately it leads to change and change is hard.
>
> —Steering Committee member

Coordinated systems of support, advanced primarily through the seven CILs as trusted community organizations implementing the BCLC vision, are at the heart of the effort to reduce African American child deaths. CILs are building a network for change within their neighborhoods and across the county. All CILs provide a wide range of services, with some more focused on youth and family services and others maintaining a broader community development agenda. To develop the infrastructure and system of services and supports needed to reduce Black child deaths, CILs leverage partnerships with community-based nonprofits, churches, schools, and business located within their respective communities. Two of the seven CILs are two faith-based organizations.

The emphasis on community partners is part of the collective impact framework employed by BCLC. These words—"community," "together" in "partnership," and "work[ing] across sectors"—appear throughout BCLC literature and annual reports. *Making Equity Happen: Year, Actions, Learnings, and Deliverables* (2019–2020), written by the CIL staff and shared with participants at the SC-RAACD retreat held in September 2019 in Berkeley, states on its first page, "The Black Child Legacy Campaign brings together members, city and county agencies, healthcare providers, community-based organizations and faith community to address the causes and disproportionate rate of African American children dying in the county."

This language is consistent with other reports and collateral material. In bold blue print the *2018 Annual Report: Growing a Community Movement* states, "The Black Child Legacy Campaign uses a collective impact approach to bring agencies and individuals across multiple sectors together to work toward a shared vision to improve outcomes for African American children in Sacramento County."

Community and collaborative efforts are also underscored in the application for presenters for the Gathering for G.L.O.R.Y.: Giving Love to Our Rising Youth Conference. It states, "With this year's theme of Building Our Beloved Community, this conference seeks to bridge wisdom, perspectives and experiences from the faith-based community to those of our Black Child Legacy Campaign communities. . . . This year's conference will focus on collaborative community-based strategies."

Community partnerships play an important role in the coordinated system. The number of community partnerships for each CIL varies. For example, the CIL in Oak Park has more than forty community partners.

CILs are required to regrant a portion of their grant funding to community partners. Known as Legacy Grants, these regrants are intended to build local capacity to support Black children and supplement CIL activities. Grant recipients are determined through a systematic review process. Other formal partnerships, including those developed with local schools or school districts, are established through Memoranda of Understanding. To reinforce these partnerships, most CILs have monthly partner meetings in which all the organizations supporting the neighborhood's campaign to reduce Black child death come together to review and coordinate their work. CILs also rely on informal partners, including volunteers and local businesses, to strengthen the network of supports they provide to families and children.

As mentioned previously, CILs and other stakeholders often worked and operated in silos within their communities before BCLC's formation. The significance of the coordinated network is best captured through participants' reflections:

> "I think for our community to come together to see that there's something outside of this neighborhood and that we can do something collectively together and make the impact that we have made, that's huge. I think that's historical for Sacramento."—community intervention worker

> "Our greatest success is the community coming together. Not just Oak Park but Meadowview, Del Paso, North Highlands. BCLC has brought everyone together."—CIL staff member

During the spring of 2020, many families in the seven neighborhoods were severely affected when Sacramento County mandated sheltering in place. The

CILs held multiple Zoom meetings to assist families with meals and other essentials. More than 50 community members and staff were on a Zoom call in April 2020 to discuss their community needs and actions taking place. The CIL staff provided updates. One participant stated, "I only have twenty minutes for the call because I have to meet the families and pass out the food." Another participant responded, "I will be right behind because we have families coming now." In addition to coordinating a network for families to receive essential services, BCLC members also spoke out against the lack of resources during COVID-19. ABC News-Sacramento featured a press conference led by Rev. Les Simmons, Kindra Montgomery-Block, and Berry Accius in which they addressed the need for resources for youth development, mental health services, violence prevention, and jobs.

With a strong focus on shared outcomes, goals, and deliverables, CILs have created both local and county-wide advocate networks. At the same time, some CIL staff mentioned in interviews that they would like more recognition of their programs and the experiences they brought to their work with BCLC, so that all progress is not attributed to BCLC. In addition, although some CILs are working closely with schools to reach youth, this connection needs to be strengthened and expanded to keep youth engaged in education—an essential strategy for reducing deaths by third-party homicide.

Insights Related to Coordinated Systems of Support

1. *Cultivating relationships with local community leaders and nonprofits builds trust* between historically marginalized communities and third-party and government agencies.

2. *CILs are providing much-needed support for nonprofits and agencies* located within the same community, allowing organizations to align their goals, review data, collaborate for events, and share information; this collaboration helps reduce administrative overlap and duplication of services.

3. *A collaborative structure* (in the form of a "link" that is "bridging the gap" or a "community connector") through which nonprofits, community leaders, county and city officials, government entities, and health organizations can focus their efforts on reducing Black child deaths is critical to collective impact.

Beyond the Numbers: Humanizing the Data

Data is essential.

—CIL staff member

The data-driven accountability and collective impact strategy has been implemented in multiple ways. Because BCLC's mission is reducing Black child deaths, statistical analyses of patterns in child deaths and the disparities between rates of Black child death and those of all other children in Sacramento County are at the core of the work. Although quantitative data neither tell the entire story nor humanize the process and work involved, data on the disproportionate rates at which Black children die in Sacramento County *have* led to a commitment to change. According to one participant, "BCLC made Black health and Black lives a high priority in Sacramento. As a result, deaths and violence has been down, and communities have been made safer." Data are not only helping communities learn and understand disparities but also giving hope to the next generation for better life outcomes.

Data are the driving force of the BCLC. The website has information about upcoming events, resources, and CIL updates. Each CIL has a link to a "Neighborhood Profile, "Education Dashboard," and "Neighborhood Crime and Safety Profile." These user-friendly profiles created and prepared by LPC Consulting Associates, Inc. make it possible for community members and CILs to have access to data specifically for their communities. Data are also the focus of each annual report. At the Sacramento County Board of Supervisors meeting in January 2019 and the RAACD retreat in September 2019 in Berkeley, data were the rallying cry and provided a reason to celebrate.

At the CIL level, implementation of strategies is assessed through progress reports their staff prepare, as well as external quality assessments. Several participants discussed the challenges of completing the reports and the advantages some CILs had because of their greater capacity and human capital. Several participants reflected on the challenges of data collection:

> "It is a struggle and we have to find the time with all that we have to do. We don't have the help but we get it done."

> "Our data sucks. We're just not good at collecting."

> "They have been collecting the data for twenty years. That's another example, I think, of institutional racism and poverty pimping because you're in these neighborhoods collecting this data and you're not analyzing it for the benefit of the neighborhood."

"Early on there was a lot of challenges in creating forms, getting them to use the forms, getting people to upload data, getting people to have the right technology to do that. We now have the database."

"Data is essential. You have to show the numbers. You have to show what you're doing for it to reflect, 'Is this impactful?'"

The Steering Committee on Reduction of African American Child Deaths has made data systems and training a priority for CILs. Recognizing that the CILs had different degrees of experience with data collection systems, The Center created a data hub with consultants who provide technical assistance and periodically update reports with neighborhood data. Although the data hub does reduce the burden of data collection, some CILs continue to feel burdened by the time it takes to input and analyze the data requested. Over the years, data systems and data collection have been streamlined; the challenge now is to establish a uniform tracking system that is user friendly, secure, and accessible. A hub data analyst discussed how collecting data has been made easier through trainings and having meetings with each CIL. After assessing each CIL's data system to determine its capabilities and capacities, the analyst acknowledged that the CILs have varying data-related strengths: "There is this big broad spectrum so we come with a blanket approach. There are some CILS with years of experience while others have tried to invest in data systems but have no funds to invest."

In addition to progress reports, the quality of the programmatic efforts of each CIL is assessed through site visits carried out by teams of four to six that include representatives from The Center, Technical Assistance providers, CIL staff, and others. Each team member uses a rubric to rate the CIL's implementation of BCLC work along dimensions such as youth engagement, community capacity building, mission focus, and communications. Site visits are held every six months and have affirmed the continued improvement in CILs' implementation of activities intended to reduce Black child death in the county.

Insights Related to Data-Driven Accountability and Collective Impact

1. *Data collection is essential, but participants need to know why they are collecting specific information.* When they have that informtion, participants gain a sense of purpose and become motivated to improve rates of infant mortality and homicide.

2. *Communities need to own the data.* Instead of using outside organizations or researchers, data should be collected and analyzed in partnership with the community being represented in/by the data.
3. *The implementation of data systems/collection must be consistent from one organization to the next.*

Implementation of these five strategies requires a community-based approach supported by resources, opportunities, and human capital. BCLC successes are the result of targeted and well-planned strategies that transform how families, community members, agencies, organizations, and institutions communicate and collaborate to advance shared goals. See table 21.1 for a summary of the lessons learned from the BCLC.

Recommendations for Other Counties and Cities

Sacramento County's success in reducing Black deaths, building an effective and well-organized network of community leaders and nonprofits across multiple neighborhoods, and advocating for policy and structural changes provides a roadmap for other regions, counties, or networks looking for effective strategies to improve the quality of life for historically marginalized communities of color. Located in Northern California, Sacramento County is the home to a majority of the state government's agencies, a major gateway to agricultural commerce, and a desirable city for new families relocating from the San Francisco–Oakland Bay Area. As a midsized liberal metropolitan area with a very diverse population positioned next to several conservative counties, Sacramento is unique. These characteristics do play a role in the successes and challenges of BCLC's strategies. Although no two cities, counties, or organizations are the same, here are four recommendations for communities interested in implementing a transformative framework:

1. *Solutions need to be systemic, consistent, and courageous.* There are no bandages that can cover up systemic racism in this country; the wounds run deep. As John Lewis taught us, "Do not get lost in a sea of despair. Be hopeful, be optimistic. Our struggle is not the struggle of a day, a week, a month, or a year; it is the struggle of a lifetime. Never ever be afraid to make some noise and get in good trouble, necessary trouble."
2. *Examine the historical context of the target communities.* Racial inequities and injustices are the result of discriminatory policies,

TABLE 21.1   Summary of lessons from the Black Child Legacy Campaign

Training and support for advocacy and community leadership are part of engaging community residents in the campaign.

➢ BCLC established the Community Leadership Roundtable for community volunteers to come together across the seven neighborhoods and gain skills and experience with advocacy for resources to reduce African American child deaths.

Public agencies must commit to the mission of reducing all child deaths, starting with addressing racial disparities in rates of death.

➢ Sacramento County and City agencies have out-stationed county staff in community-based organizations and supported staff partnership with local nonprofit service providers.

➢ BCLC continues to work toward the creation of a public entity that will be responsible for children's well-being and health equity in the county.

A coordinated system of support for the reduction of Black child death requires trusted, capable neighborhood organizations taking the lead; partnership with other county and local agencies; and an entity that serves as a connector and backbone for the work.

➢ BCLC is implemented through seven Community Incubator Leads, which are trusted, local nonprofit organizations that are responsible for coordinating efforts in each of the neighborhoods.

➢ The intimate connection with the local community affected by child deaths and its relationship with county agencies are making it easier for social services and community leaders to work together.

➢ BCLC's collaborative structure has been facilitated by The Center, a nonprofit backbone organization that is responsible for distributing funding, facilitating learning, driving communications, ensuring accountability, and providing other supports.

Communications are key to building a movement toward a common goal.

➢ The name "Black Child Legacy Campaign" challenges deficit paradigms steeped in anti-Blackness and as a result is a powerful and inspired public call for action.

➢ Promotion of BCLC through swag gear/materials, such as scarves, posters, and t-shirts, at public events and forums focuses awareness of the urgent issues facing the African American community.

Data and measurable goals for the reduction of deaths keep the work focused and mission driven.

➢ The targets set for reduction of African American child deaths and the regular reporting of progress toward those targets have given BCLC participants a sense of purpose and motivation.

➢ Regular quality assessments of the work at the neighborhood level have helped the community lead agencies strengthen their strategies for reducing African American child deaths.

practices, and processes. Each of the seven communities served by BCLC has a unique history, but they share common threads of divestment and neglect that help explain why these contexts evolved into spaces hostile to the lives of African American children.

3. *Any new plan, strategy, or action should be inclusive, equitable, and antiracist.* Local residents, organizations, activists, and leaders should have as much say, influence, and decision-making authority as elected

official, policy makers, and funders. Community-driven initiatives depend on the belief that "we are all in this together" and the future depends on every member in the community.

4. *Alongside strategic advocacy, the dollars need to make sense; do not examine any one cause in isolation.* Political pressure from a wide range of stakeholders is imperative: it holds those in power accountable to the genuine needs of the people. For example, when BCLC received an additional two million dollars from the City of Sacramento, it was a win. But relative to the overall city budget (say, for instance, the amount provided to law enforcement), this funding underscores that the struggle over equitable and preventable resources is still contentious. How does Black health and well-being connect to white privilege and property? An intersectional analysis fortifies a stronger bridge to racial justice.

Building a Legacy for Black Families

> There [are] so many issues that need to be addressed but little resources . . . We need more time. 2020 is here and there is going to be so much work to do. We must continue past 2020 and work toward sustainability.
>
> —MDT staff

> The future of BCLC and its sustainable depends on County's support. What happens next?
>
> —MDT staff

In the year 2020, Black Lives Matter became a global cry and urgent call for justice, equity, the defunding of school resource officers, and the end of racial violence toward Black people all over the world. Demands to end racist policies that were producing racial inequities in health care, education, criminal justice, employment, and housing prompted a deep examination of institutional and systemic oppression. As the movement carries forward, the words of Dr. Martin Luther King Jr. continues to ring loud: "Where do we go from here?"

The Black Child Legacy Campaign's community-driven efforts and collective impact model are examples of what should be coming next and what the future holds for Black communities across the United States. From its inception, its mission was to protect and support the growth of Black children. Saving the lives of Black children remained central through BCLC's process of forming its steering committee, outlining goals and outcomes, selecting the seven neighborhoods, and determining strategies and priorities. Intentionally selecting the word "legacy" in its name connected the present to the future as the work took place in the present. The collective action of the SC-RAAD, CILs, cultural brokers, crisis intervention, community partners, and Sacramento County and City of Sacramento agencies ensured that the ground was stable for the present generation to prosper in the years to come. In the *Black Child Legacy Campaign Five Year Report* (2020) Chet Hewitt states, "We've created home-grown infrastructure that can continue to serve communities, save lives, and build more promising futures."

Future Forward

> What is the legacy you're trying to leave for black children in Sacramento? They can expect to live a life of hope, peace and have longevity.
>
> —CIL member

What is next for the Black Child Legacy Campaign? Being future forward means not merely moving but also requires intentional and strategic thinking and planning for the next ten to twenty years to affirm that *futures matter* for Black children and their families (Winn 2019).

What is meant by being future forward in the context of BCLC? Here, we argue that it is imperative to imagine possible lives while working to liberate the public from fatalistic renderings of Black children and Black lives. Futures forward is embedded in the name "Black Child Legacy." The decision to focus on legacies as opposed to mortality is key here. As we imagine the future of BCLC, we think about the year 2032. What is the preferred future of BCLC and Sacramento? What is needed to create this preferred future? The portraits of stakeholders in this book provide a mapping of assets and identify areas of growth that need to be addressed to move BCLC in this direction. Can we get to this place? The answer is yes.

NOTE

1. For example: "Black Infant Death Rates down in Sacramento following Massive Community Efforts," Capitol Public Radio, December 3, 2018; "For the First Time in 35 Years, No Children Were Murdered in the City of Sacramento Last Year," CBS Sacramento, January 21, 2019; and "Teen Homicides Fall to Zero as Sacramento Sees Overall Decline in Murders in 2019," *Sacramento Bee*, January 28, 2020.

REFERENCES

Kendi, Ibram X. 2019. *How to Be an Antiracist.* New York: Random House/One World.

Neely, P. 2019. "Sacramento Is Reducing Black Child Deaths: Here Is What LA Can Learn." KPCC-FM, July 29. https://www.scpr.org/news/2019/07/29/90390/sacramento-is-reducing-black-child-deaths-here-s-w/.

Winn, Maisha T. 2018. *Justice on Both Sides: Transforming Education through Restorative Justice.* Cambridge, MA: Harvard Education Press.

Winn, Maisha T. 2019. *Paradigm Shift in Teacher Education.* Ann Arbor: University of Michigan TeachingWorks.

A REOPENING

Futures Forward

Vajra M. Watson

There is a word in South Africa—*ubuntu*—that reflects the idea that humanity is bound together in ways that are invisible to the eye yet are gripping to the soul: it is a oneness that inspires compassion and invites connection. The word *ubuntu* is part of the Zulu phrase *Umuntu ngumuntu ngabantu*, which literally means that a person is a person through other people. This kind of ontology of collectivity imbues a milieu of *we-our* togetherness, deeply rooted to the African philosophy of *I am because we are*. Not to be confused with kumbaya colorblindness, it is a radical understanding that one person's hunger can lead us all to starve.

Our interdependence is real, yet it can be hard to see. Unity, even harder to achieve.

Intentional integrity demands a reckoning with our present reality and the tensions between ethics and actuality. As a society, we must be courageous enough to honestly reflect on our histories and the deleterious epigenetics of white supremacy. At the local level, we tried to do this in Sacramento.

Living together in a city is relational, cultural, material, and spiritual; it is beautiful and complicated. Neighborhoods are created (and destroyed) through various policies and politics, but that does not tell the entirety of the human story because places are made up of people. Throughout this book, we aimed to cultivate a nuanced, multidimensional portrait of a county told through the individuals on the frontlines of the Black Child Legacy Campaign (BCLC). To create an accurate rendering of this enduring coalition, we rooted the work in communities of praxis.

Applying Maisha T. Winn's (2018) transformative justice framework to the BCLC research generated insights necessary to our overarching analysis. Let's take a moment to revisit how mattering shaped and informed our study:

- **History matters**: The history of Sacramento was carefully scrutinized to understand how and why current disparities exist.
- **Race matters**: The county examined their data, giving particular attention to racial disparities. This explicit focus on race and racism provided a catalyst to do the work and centralize the health and well-being of Black children and youth.
- **Language matters**: Words reflect our visions of the world. The name change from *Reducing Black Deaths* to the *Black Child Legacy* Campaign signified an important shift in assets, aspirations, and purpose.
- **Justice matters**: The quest for justice echoes throughout the data; it is the commitment to do the work and love Black families and communities publicly, unapologetically, and courageously.
- **Futures matter**: The Black Child Legacy Campaign continues to reimagine the possibilities of Sacramento. Centering our children is significant: as the elders say, *If you want to know the future, walk alongside the children.*

Each component of mattering shed a particular ray of light on the movement-building efforts and grounded our findings. Altogether, what emerged are humanizing testimonies that heal, restore, and make whole. Although repairing harm is individual and interpersonal, it also needs to be institutional.

Remembrance and Reparations

The Black Child Legacy Campaign was launched with a multimillion-dollar investment from the Sacramento County Board of Supervisors. Money matters, and when paired with a strong infrastructure, can support sustainable improvements. BCLC proved to be a county-based solution, but how would strategic funding at the state level shape the material conditions of African American communities?

California has a unique and powerful opportunity to serve as a model for the nation. In 2020, Governor Gavin Newsom established the country's first state-level reparations task force to study and develop proposals that would provide resources to African Americans because of slavery. This initiative prompts us to face the past and understand how inequalities are designed and perpetuated. Although we cannot change history, we can understand it and not repeat it.

It is well known that chattel slavery was the world's largest economic operation, built solely on the stealing, selling, and ownership of Black bodies as legal property from 1619 to 1865. By 1860, "the nearly 4 million American slaves were worth some $3.5 billion, making them the largest single financial asset in the entire U.S. economy, worth more than all manufacturing and railroads combined" (Coates 2014). Although it is difficult to quantify the sheer immensity and intergenerational gravity of slavery, there have been attempts to do so. For example, in January of 1865, *Field Order 15* promised formerly enslaved Africans 400,000 acres of land that stretched from South Carolina to Florida. However, four months later, the order was rescinded.

Given the pervasiveness of anti-Black racism in this country, it is shameful that the United States has not acknowledged or sought to repair hundreds of years of systemic oppression, especially when there is legal precedent to do it. Consider that from 1934 to 1941, the Indian Reorganization Act authorized $2 million a year for the reacquisition of land, totaling one million acres.[1] The Civil Liberties Act of 1988 granted reparations to Japanese Americans who were forced into internment camps from 1942 to 1946. North Carolina now pays reparations to living survivors of the state's eugenics program that forcibly sterilized more than 7,600 people between 1929 and 1974.[2] The nonprofit organization, Jewish Material Claims Against Germany, continues to secure material compensation for Jewish Holocaust survivors. To date, the German government has paid more than $90 billion to individuals who were persecuted by Nazis from 1933 to 1945.[3]

Reparations for African Americans continues to be a dream deferred, but it is not impossible. Some places are trying to reconcile with their past. In Virginia, counties that were pro-segregation closed schools to boycott the *Brown vs. Board of Education* ruling. As a result, a generation of Black children, who are now fifty to sixty years old, lost the opportunity to attend school. The state of Virginia is paying reparations to all these individuals.[4]

As another beacon of hope, in 2019, students at Georgetown University voted to increase their own tuition by $27.20 per student per semester to benefit the descendants of the 272 enslaved Africans who were sold to provide the funds to establish the university. In addition, applicants who are the offspring of these African Americans receive preference in admissions. The school formally acknowledged its role in slavery and has sought to make amends.[5]

Harkening back to 1857, Frederick Douglass' speech about struggling towards racial justice relate to contemporary debates about reparations. He saw a different America on the horizon and implored us to keep fighting:

If there is no struggle there is no progress.
Those who profess to favor freedom and yet deprecate agitation
are [people] who want crops without plowing up the ground;
they want rain without thunder and lightning.
They want the ocean without the awful roar of its many waters.
This struggle may be a moral one,
or it may be a physical one,
and it may be both moral and physical,
but it must be a struggle.
Power concedes nothing without a demand.
It never did and it never will.[6]

Now, it is February of 2023, and Secretary of State Shirley Weber is at Sacramento State University discussing Assembly Bill 3121, the groundbreaking legislation that demands reparations for Black Californians. Inside this campus auditorium full of faculty, staff, and students, Weber explains that the State of California is the "fourth-largest economy in the world" and can "afford to apologize with actions." There is growing momentum for AB 3121, and time will tell. To say that reparations for Black people in this country is a long time coming is an understatement; it should have occurred yesterday.

Crossroads

While beacons of Black leadership illuminate a way forward, that is not the only road. I wish I could write that the journey is always just, but there is another path. A lineage laid in bone and poured with blood. A walk in the world that is fear-induced and suffocates, marked with preventable deaths and death ends. It is, in the words of our friend and colleague Rich Milner, "woke without work" and just plain sleep. Current legislation like the "Stop WOKE Act" literally impedes learning. Right now, it is illegal to teach AP African American Studies in Florida[7] and a teacher in Tennessee was fired for showing a video about white privilege to his students.[8] These contemporary attacks on civil rights reveal a hard truth: the Eurocentric logic of colonization, censorship, and control still exists and is gaining traction.

My son asked me point-blank: Will white supremacy take the world with it? And I ask: Can our humanity thrive in a state of violence, inequality, and selfish pursuits? No. We will not. We cannot. There must be another way forward.

Freedom Dreaming

Sacramento is not a lost or hopeless place; rather, it is a sociopolitical ecosystem struggling between oppression and liberation. Sometimes, people can agree ideologically and still not achieve equitable results. Unfortunately, siloes and bureaucracies can fuel divisions. Is the City Council member breaking bread with the community activist? Can the poet and the police chief find common purpose? The Black Child Legacy Campaign provided incentives to work together in new ways. And throughout this process, individuals got to know one another beyond institutional barriers and built authentic connections for racial justice.

In 2020, as the world was turning inward because of the COVID-19 pandemic, BCLC leaders like Timothy Poole, Tanya Bean-Garrett, Les Simmons, Berry Accius, Cassandra Jennings, Tina Roberts, and countless others in Sacramento were reaching outward and across the aisle. Low-income African American families were among the hardest hit by COVID-19, and the BCLC was able to pivot its programming and galvanize crisis response teams that took the following actions:

> Organizing food pickup stations during quarantine
>
> Leading community peace walks throughout every hood to keep people connected
>
> Offering creative healing sessions over Zoom to help families mourn together the loss of their children
>
> Strategically securing new sources of funding, such as emergency rental assistance to those who lost their jobs so that they would not also lose their homes

These were just some of the tangible solutions—byproducts of collaboration and a larger quest for beloved community.

However, although these efforts are real and inspirational, it would be irresponsible to act as if Sacramento has fixed its problems. There is nothing romantic about the painful realities of oppression. African American leaders in our city persist amidst onslaughts of injustice and preventable deaths. Black mothers and Black babies are still not safe. A new study published by the National Bureau of Economic Research (2023) found that, regardless of wealth, childbirth in California is deadlier for Black families.[9] And even when children survive, racism saturates our systems. Sacramento, like so many regions across this country, continues to grapple with vast health disparities and youth violence. In April 2022, gunfire erupted in our downtown area that left six people dead (two of whom were only twenty-one years old).

Grief and trauma weigh heavy inside the heart of a neighborhood forced to bury its young. As documented in previous chapters, third-party homicides ceased for a while, but it is important to acknowledge that they have not stopped. Tears continue to amass. Death tolls amass. Funerals amass. I am not here to close our journey with melancholy, but to offer a sobering reminder that we are still wailing. If agony is not treated, it can metastasize and pathologize into various ailments of nihilism. Mental health and wellness investments are needed for the community and for those who hold the community. Healers need healing too.

Doing this kind of work can be exhausting not just to the body but also in the soul. Tricia Hersey (2022) provides a healing balm in *Rest Is Resistance*. She asserts, "Rest, in its simplest form, becomes an act of resistance and a reclaiming of power because it asserts our most basic humanity. We are enough. The systems cannot have us." Amidst the barrage of demands, there is power in the pause. So, even though the fight for justice is nonstop, we will not experience justice unless we stop. Building on this sentiment, poet Nikki Giovanni reminds us, "Sometimes the window is open and a breeze comes through singing a sweet song: it is nap time. Grandmother sits on the front porch; grandpapa cuts the grass. It is a song. You nap. I nap. The angels hug us."[10] Rest is resistance, and it is also revolutionary. Rest can literally reignite us. Without rest, how will we, in the words of Robin Kelley (2002), *freedom dream*?

As if answering this call to freedom dream, the New Orleans artist, Brandan "BMike" Odums, created the phrase, *I am my ancestors' wildest dreams*. This sentiment reaches into the soul of the Black Child Legacy Campaign. In Sacramento, BCLC continues to be co-created through multiple lifelines. Individual efforts are intricately connected across time, just like how a single tree can multiply into a forest. Sacramento is deemed the "City of Trees" and has the potential to leave lessons that grow exponentially. Essentially, BCLC embodies a long, intergenerational tradition of freedom dreaming and freedom fighting.

Radical love gives birth to radical work. From this movement we learn that there is not one single leader, one finding, or one magic bullet that signifies the solution. Rather, the answer is plural and prophetic. A mixed-methods study on intersectional organizing that centered Black people, Black power, and Black prayers. *Faith made Flesh* sees the future and reminds the children that improving the world is our sacred birthright.

> Our love for the circle of life is taught to our children
> as we live our ancestors' teachings daily.
> We are all leaders
> and when we come to the end of our earthly pathways of life,

we turn around and see what we have taught our children . . .

we will either smile or we will weep . . .

our pathways,

our imprints,

our history

will live through the ones we leave behind.

—Great-grandmother Mary Lyons, *Leech Lake Band of Ojibwe*[11]

As we continue to show up and stand tall in this work,

we look to the future as the future is calling us forward.

—Patrice Hill, Director of Sacramento Area Youth Speaks (SAYS)

NOTES

1. The 1934 Indian Reorganization Act, an attempt to provide land back to Indigenous nations, see https://www.govinfo.gov/content/pkg/COMPS-5299/pdf/COMPS-5299.pdf.

2. A eugenics program of forced sterilization focused on reducing the Black population. Read more at https://www.newsobserver.com/news/state/north-carolina/article244 411987.html.

3. The Claims Conference has conducted seven surveys across six countries examining the Jewish Holocaust and repercussions worldwide. This site also provides answers about how to obtain reparations: https://www.claimscon.org/survivor-services/comp -faqs.

4. In 1964, a ruling by the Supreme Court forced local officials to reopen schools for *all* children. However, by this time, many Black children of the 1950s in Virginia had missed out on an education. See https://www.nytimes.com/2005/07/31/education/a -new-hope-for-dreams-suspended-by-segregation.html.

5. While students voted to increase their tuition for reparations, it is unclear what the school itself is paying as a way to reconcile with its financial benefits from slavery. See https://www.nytimes.com/2019/04/12/us/georgetown-reparations.html.

6. The full speech by Douglass is written: https://www.blackpast.org/african -american-history/1857-frederick-douglass-if-there-no-struggle-there-no-progress/.

7. There are trends across the country to erase race from the curriculum. This *New York Times* article discusses the banning of AP African American Studies in Florida: https:// www.nytimes.com/2023/01/21/us/florida-ap-african-american-studies.html.

8. Similarly, this article in *The Atlantic* explains how a teacher was fired for discussing white privilege: https://www.theatlantic.com/politics/archive/2021/08/matt-hawn -tennessee-teacher-fired-white-privilege/619770/.

9. The New York Times shared findings that clearly documents disproportionate Black birth rates in California (irrespective of economic status): https://www.nytimes .com/interactive/2023/02/12/upshot/child-maternal-mortality-rich-poor.html.

10. The description of *Rest Is Resistance* and Giovanni's endorsement are listed here: https://www.hachettebookgroup.com/titles/tricia-hersey/rest-is-resistance/978031 6365536/.

11. To learn more about the life and lessons of Mary Lyons, please visit: https:// rainbowofbeing.wordpress.com/videos-1-8/mary-lyons/.

REFERENCES

Kelley, Robin. D. 2002. *Freedom Dreams: The Black Radical Imagination*. Boston: Beacon Press.

Ta-Nehisi Coates. 2014. "Slavery Made America," *The Atlantic*, June 24, 2014. https://www.theatlantic.com/business/archive/2014/06/slavery-made-america/373288/.

Hersey, Tricia. 2022. *Rest is Resistance: A Manifesto*. New York: Little, Brown Spark.

National Bureau of Economic Research. 2023. "Maternal and Infant Health Inequality: New Evidence from Linked Administrative Data" by Kennedy-Moulton, Miller, Persson, Rossin-Slater, Wherry, and Aldana. DOI 10.3386/w30693.

Winn, Maisha T. 2018. *Justice on Both Sides: Transforming Education through Restorative Justice*. Cambridge, MA: Harvard Education Press.

Contributors

Quadir Chouteau, a first-year college student at Louisiana State University, is a warrior-scholar, artist, and athlete from Sacramento. He has been rapping and performing since the age of four and is known for his charismatic personality and stellar performances. Quadir belongs to New Home Missionary Baptist Church where he serves as an active member of the drama ministry and youth choir. While serving in these ministries, he starred as Terrence Roberts of the "Little Rock Nine" and reenacted President Obama's inaugural speech in the play "The Dream Team," which debuted at the Crocker Art Museum Black History Month celebration. Quadir also starred as Young Jason & Kid in the autobiographical play, "We've Been Sentenced," for which he received the Best Debut Actor award. He placed in the top three in the SAYS (Sacramento Area Youth Speaks) MC Olympics and received a standing ovation at the California State Fair for his lead rap performance during his choir's set. In 2016, Quadir was recognized by the White House for his outstanding achievements in academics. He is a two-time champion in the 12u Bay Valley division with the Burbank Jr. Titans. He recently received the student-athlete award at Luther Burbank High in recognition of his 3.6 GPA and graduated top of his class in 2022 in the International Baccalaureate (IB) Program.

Kenneth Duncan Jr. comes from a strong line of leaders. One of his grandfathers was a professional boxer in San Francisco, and the other was a general in the U.S. Army. Whether it was their values such as dedication, discipline, sacrifice, and a sense of civic responsibility or their service to others, Kenneth had plenty of great examples to emulate.

An athlete from a very young age, Kenneth eventually landed at historic Merritt College in Oakland and the College of Alameda where he earned his associate of arts degree and played on the basketball team. From his time at the College of Alameda, Kenneth earned an athletic scholarship to attend Wilberforce University in Ohio, which is the oldest, private, Black-owned institution in the country. There he received his bachelor's degree in psychology. Kenneth is HBCU proud!

Professionally, Kenneth has worked in the nonprofit world for more than ten years. He began his career with the Boys and Girls Clubs of Greater Sacramento where he served New Helvetia and Seavey Circle public housing in Sacramento, which is now known as Marina Vista/Alder Grove. There he was able to mentor hundreds of young people and to build relationships in the community, becoming a trusted leader and advocate. His journey in Sacramento has included community organizing in Oak Park and Del Paso Heights through the BCLC. Kenneth has also worked for the Greater Sacramento Urban League, Roberts Family Development Center, and the Anti-Recidivism Coalition. In addition to serving the community through long-standing organizations in Sacramento, Kenneth has founded his own nonprofit organization, called Ball Out Academy, where he provides mentorship, leadership development, workshops, and training through the lens of athletic development programs. Kenneth plans to continue his service to the community as he expands the reach and impact of Ball Out Academy.

Kindra F. Montgomery-Block enters her second season as the vice president of diversity, inclusion, and social impact with the Sacramento Kings, following more than twenty years in community impact work. Before joining the Kings, Montgomery-Block led a number of initiatives at Sierra Health Foundation including the Black Child Legacy Campaign and Steering Committee on the Reduction of African American Child Deaths, helping dramatically lower health disparity across ethnicities and founding a new community and economic development department.

Montgomery-Block holds a master of public administration degree from Golden Gate University, a BA in political science from the University of California, Riverside, and a certificate in business communication from Harvard University. She has twice been named one of Northern California's Exceptional Women of Color by *HUB Magazine* and is the recipient of honors from Women of Color in Maternal Health, NAACP, American Association of Public Administrators, *Comstock's Magazine*, and the Greater Sacramento Urban League. She serves on a statewide Black maternal health roundtable, the California Black Freedom Fund Advisory Board, and the Sacramento County Mental Health Board of Directors. Montgomery-Block resides in Sacramento with her husband and daughter, Samone.

Damany Morris Fisher, a native of Sacramento, earned an MA and PhD in history from the University of California, Berkeley. His research investigates the origins of residential segregation in Sacramento and the fair housing movement of the 1950s–1960s. A dedicated educator, Fisher has built a career working in service of students in secondary and higher ed settings. He taught history at Mt. San Antonio College in Walnut, California; served as a member of the teaching faculty at Phillips Academy Andover in Andover, Massachusetts; and lectured inside the California State Prison Solano and the Correctional Medical Facility in Vacaville, California, as part of the Solano Community College's Corrections Education Program. Fisher currently works as a management consulting manager for Accenture.

David Blanco Gonzalez was born in Brooklyn, New York, in 1981 and moved to the Oak Park neighborhood of Sacramento when he was three years old. He began drawing as a young child, tracing character images he would receive from his father in prison. By his teenage years, hip-hop was influencing everything in his life, and he was heavily into graffiti art. In his twenties he became fascinated with the art of tattooing and got an apprenticeship at a local tattoo shop where he first put paint to canvas. Drawing inspiration from Justin Bua, Andy Warhol, and, most of all, Jean Michel Basquiat, Gonzalez created his first collection called "Legacy" to pay respect to the victims of third-party homicide in Sacramento.

Heather Gonzalez currently serves as a director for the Mutual Assistance Network. With more than fifteen years of service within the greater Sacramento area, she has demonstrated an unwavering resolve to rectify historical and continuing organizational, institutional, and systemic inequities, with an emphasis on racial equity. She considers her life's work to be rooted in antiracism action by way of education and system change. Over the years she has functioned as an organizational leader and a co-conspirator, aligned in values of antiracism and social justice to bridge systemic gaps within organizations, systems, and institutions. Gonzalez's professional focus lies in the fields of child abuse and neglect prevention, violence prevention, racial equity, and family support services, and she has specialized concentrations in the practice of harm reduction, substance abuse, and addictions treatment. Her most important role is being a wife to her amazing husband and mother to her two beautiful children.

Patrice Hill is a poet and celebrated teaching artist, with more than two decades of experience teaching in urban, suburban, and exurban classrooms. Hill currently serves as the director of Sacramento Area Youth Speaks (SAYS), which strives to change the world through education and empowerment. SAYS is recognized as a national leader in social justice-based arts education organizations, connecting the university, K–12 schools, and the community. Hill specializes in establishing distinguished partnerships between the university and school districts, providing direct service to students, developing culturally relevant curriculum, and facilitating high-level professional development trainings for teacher + youth practitioners. Hill was recently honored with a California Senate Resolution for empowering youth through poetry and social justice, while playing a pivotal role in establishing Sacramento as the poetry capital of California. Patrice Hill's greatest victory is serving and standing alongside the beautiful and brilliant youth in Sacramento and beyond.

Patrice Hill identifies as a Black, cisgender female.

Adiyah Ma'at Obolu is a current senior at Inderkum High School. She is passionate about racial justice and how equity can be actualized in education. She is a part of many organizations that bring these challenges alive: she is the chief of staff of the College to Career Ready (CCR) team, the president of the Black Student Union (BSU), and student body president. Adiyah is an avid poet and uses this art form to inspire and heal. As a social justice warrior, she actively yearns to reimagine society through the lens of radical love.

Adiyah Obolu identifies as a Black, cisgender female.

Amaya Noguera-Mujica is a program officer at the Sierra Health Foundation. She has extensive experience in education, community organizing, and culturally responsive program development for historically underserved communities. Noguera-Mujica is committed to fighting injustice and advocating for communities that have been marginalized and disadvantaged. She currently oversees the Community Responsive Wellness Program in Sacramento, which centers holistic health and wellness for healing in serving Black Communities. She received her BA degree in educational theory from New School University in 2007 and has received national acclaim and awards for her work as a writer and organizer, and for her commitment to community service and social change. A dedicated mother, Noguera-Mujica has had opportunities to expand on this work in the Caribbean and Central and South America.

Ijeoma Ononuju earned a PhD in education, with an emphasis on language, literacy, and culture. A 2010–2011 McNair cohort scholar, he has a devotion to youth, families, and community. Born and raised in Vallejo, California, Ononuju continues to positively affect and inform the educational experiences of young people through his research and service. He is currently the assistant director of the Graduate School of Education at Touro University, California. Ononuju also co-created *BlackademX*, a weekly podcast engaging educators across the nation in critical dialogue about academic success for African American scholars.

Vanessa Segundo is a research and evaluation associate consultant at Mirror Group LLC, where she designs culturally responsive and racially equitable evaluations and strategies to support organizational transformation. Before becoming a consultant, she worked at the intersection of student affairs, research, and teaching for twelve years. Segundo is a proud daughter of immigrant parents, a first-generation college graduate, and *Mami* to two beloved little humans. She is from Chicago, a city that fuels her passion to design child-centered futures. Segundo received her BA from the University of Illinois at Chicago, her MsEd from Northern Illinois University, and her PhD in education from the University of California, Davis.

Segundo identifies as a Latina, cisgender female.

Vajra M. Watson is a scholar activist, faculty director, and professor of educational leadership and racial justice in the College of Education at Sacramento State University. Watson has more than twenty years of experience as a teacher, community organizer, and researcher. She is the founder of Sacramento Area Youth Speaks (SAYS), an award-winning program that pairs community-based poet-mentor educators and teachers to develop grassroots pedagogies that reclaim and reimagine schooling. She is the author of three books, *Learning to Liberate: Community-Based Solutions to the Crisis in Urban Education* (2012), *Transformative Schooling: Towards Racial Equity in Education* (2018), and *The Soul of Learning: Rituals of Resistance, Magnetic Pedagogy and Living Justice* (co-authored with Mary Keator, 2022). She has published dozens of peer-reviewed journal articles and book chapters. Watson serves on several boards, including United Playaz in San Francisco (board president), People's Think Tank, and Kingmakers of Oakland (board cochair). Watson is a recipient of Sacramento's 40 under 40 Leadership Award, the California Educational Research Association's Annual Award, the Congressional Woman of the Year Award, and the American Educational Research Association's Social Impact Award and Social Justice Leadership Award. She is originally from Berkeley, California, and was deeply affected by the courses she took in the Black and Xicanx Studies Departments at Berkeley High School in the mid-1990s. In tenth grade her final exam question was, "What are you doing to stop and/or curtail the spread of white supremacy in yourself, community, and this world?" This question still shapes her path and purpose. Watson received her BA from UC Berkeley and her doctorate in administration, planning, and social policy from the Graduate School of Education at Harvard University.

Watson identifies as a white, cisgender female.

Lawrence "Torry" Winn is an associate professor of Teaching in Education in the School of Education at the University of California, Davis, and the cofounder and executive director of the Transformative Justice in Education (TJE) Center. His program of research examines race, critical consciousness, and social capital in out-of-school learning spaces and transformative justice pedagogy and practice within schools. A trained ethnographer, Winn is interested in the relationship and dynamics between historically marginalized communities of color and schools, nonprofits, and government entities such as police, elected officials, and policy makers. He has more than two decades of experience in the nonprofit sector, including work with Casey Family Programs and the Annie E. Casey Foundation. Winn was also a member of the Race to Equity Team (R2E) that published *Race to Equity Report*, a comprehensive study of racial disparities in education, criminal justice, the workforce, and health care for Black and white families in Dane County, Wisconsin. He is the coauthor of articles appearing in *Theory into Practice*, *Race and Social Problems*, and *Adolescent Research Review*.

Torry Winn identifies as a Black, cisgender male.

Maisha T. Winn is the associate dean and Chancellor's Leadership Professor in the School of Education at the University of California, Davis, where she cofounded and co-directs (with Dr. Lawrence "Torry" Winn) the Transformative Justice in Education (TJE) Center. Much of Professor Winn's early scholarship examines how young people create literate identities through performing literacy and how teachers who are "practitioners of the craft" serve as "soul models" to emerging writers. Most recently, she has examined how restorative justice theory can be leveraged to teach across disciplines using a transformative justice teacher education framework. Winn was named an American Educational Research Association Fellow in 2016. In 2014 she received the William T. Grant Foundation Distinguished Fellowship and was named the American Educational Research Association Early Career Award recipient in 2012. Winn served as the Jeannette K. Watson Distinguished Visiting Professor in the Humanities at Syracuse University for the 2019–2020 academic year. She is the author of several books including *Writing in Rhythm: Spoken Word Poetry in Urban Schools* (published under her maiden name "Fisher"); *Black Literate Lives: Historical and Contemporary Perspectives* (published under her maiden name "Fisher"); and *Girl Time: Literacy, Justice, and the School-to-Prison Pipeline*; she is the coeditor of *Humanizing Research: Decolonizing Qualitative Research* (with Django Paris). Winn's most recent books are *Justice on Both Sides: Transforming Education through Restorative Justice* and *Restorative Justice in the English Language Arts Classroom* (with Hannah Graham and Rita Alfred). She is also the author of numerous articles in peer-reviewed journals.

Maisha Winn identifies as a Black, cisgender female.

Index

Note: Illustrations and tables are indicated by page numbers in *italics*.

.

www.ingramcontent.com/pod-product-compliance
Lightning Source LLC
Chambersburg PA
CBHW030820270326
41928CB00007B/822